W9-DDV-037

The Reckonings of Red Knech
Book III

Zan and the Mythical Art of Miz-Management

by James Alden

Produced by:

FriesenPress

Suite 300 – 852 Fort Street
Victoria, BC, Canada V8W 1H8

www.friesenpress.com

Distributed to the trade by The Ingram Book Company

Dedication

This book is dedicated to my wonderful and beautiful wife, Carmen, not only for all her support, but for her amazing 'Carmen Sense,' all evidence of which has been carefully edited out of the content of this book to avoid logic, ensure inconsistency, and maximize the reader's *Miz-Experience*.

I would have also loved to include the names of those inspirational fellow employees, colleagues, and managers with whom I have had the happenstance to contend with in the workplace. I owe a real debt of gratitude to all of them, as they are the real models of behaviour for the eight characteristics outlined in this book. However, my lawyer has advised against naming them to avoid any potential lawsuits.

Despite my best efforts to create a tedious work and avoid the application of wit or humour, it appears that some of the content may have inadvertently been interpreted otherwise. I believe I can reasonably attribute this to the corrupting influence of some of my dear coffee colleagues and friends. I would very much like to acknowledge each of them personally for their valueless contributions; however, I'm obliged to defer to their request to be unequivocally disassociated with this manuscript, as I've already spent the money they contributed to ensure their anonymity. The one exception is my good friend Mark, not because his contribution is still lost somewhere in the mail, but because I just couldn't bear to hurt his feeling.

James

PS: I would also like to sincerely thank my editor, Warren Layberry, and the *Concise Oxford Dictionary, Ninth Edition*.

An introduction to Book III
Zan and the Mythical Art of Miz-Management

In order to appreciate the subtleties embedded in this treatise, a clear understanding of the meaning of the title might be helpful. Unfortunately, it is not. However, it is presented here anyway, so let's start with the key word; *Miz-Management*. *Miz* is a contraction of the word miserable, which is what masochists strive to be. The Oxford Dictionary defines masochism as *'a form of perversion characterized by gratification derived from one's own pain or humiliation, or the enjoyment of what appears to be painful or tiresome.'* Therefore, *Miz-Management* simply means miserable management for masochists. The suggestions on management behaviour outlined in this book are in support of the principles of *Miz-Management* and the theoretical methodology for creating an ideal state of *Mizery* in the workplace, known as a *Miz-Environment*.

Many masochists may feel that reading this book will have little or nothing to offer: however, it might be worth reconsidering this position simply for the sheer torture of enduring yet another volume of incompetent literature. While there are numerous easier methods for a person with masochistic tendencies to achieve gratification from pain or humiliation, most are not very imaginative. For example, being poor, taking drugs, gambling, living in an abusive relationship, having children, and entering politics are but a few of these rudimentary insipid practices. A creative masochist, on the other hand, finds little or no expediency in these choices and may look for more challenging opportunities to realize genuine *Mizery*, such as reading this book.

To provide assistance to the somewhat less intellectually advanced masochists or more importantly to the closet *Mizzies*, a detailed explanation might be in order, especially since it will be quite useless. While the purpose of this book remains vague, it is likely irrelevant for a manuscript that is attempting to outline largely unproven methodologies, supported by unimaginative examples of *Miz-Management*. It is concocted specifically for those who want to be perceived as trying to improve their management skills but who really want to be anything but successful.

So… one may ask, what possible market could there be for a book on *Miz-Management*? Is it not ludicrous to think that there is anyone out there who might deliberately want to make their lives more *Mizerable* than they already are? Is it not even more absurd to imagine that some might be willing to pay for a book on the subject? Well, I too once held the position that confused thinking, errors, or even bad luck were behind most of the strange management decisions and actions that so often resulted in conditions of *Mizery* and failure. However, the number of people who love being insulted by Don Rickles and the reckonings of Mr. Red Knech have now corrected my naïve notion on this perspective.

The word *Art,* which serves no real purpose, has been inserted to add a sense of pretentious intellectualism, and also, it sounds better than *knack*. Next, we have the word *Mythical,* which has been included for the many skeptics out there who are still of the opinion that *Mizzies* are mythical creatures who don't exist in the real world. It replaces my original choice – '*mystical*,' which unfortunately has too many positive associations, such as The Beatles' *Magical Mystery Tour,* and therefore may be deemed to send the wrong message.

Finally, let's return to the first word 'Zan.' Some may assume that this is simply a misspelling of the word Zen, but that's not it at all. Actually it's a nickname for the name Alexandra. That was Red's first wife's name, and although he didn't really appreciate it at the time, life with Zan was a euphoric state of *Mizery,* known as a *Miz-State*. The point is that every *Mizzy* needs their own personal 'Zan' to bring meaningful and constant *Mizery* into their lives.

While the stratagem is to generate frustration and annoyance anonymously to perpetuate the condition indefinitely, there are two notes of caution that must be pointed out. The first is that if your company goes under, you may find yourself in a similar position to the parasite that kills its host. The other is less obvious but considerably more noteworthy and is probably the most common failure in the field of *Miz-Management*. It is a condition where a *Miz-Manager* finds that, after working hard to establish a highly effective *Miz-Environment*, they are not reaping sufficient beneficial misery from their strenuous efforts. Here they are, surrounded by frustration and demoralization, and yet they find themselves in the ironic position of being personally insulated from all this delightful pain and suffering. After all that effort, how could this happen?

The problem seems to be that these *Miz-Managers* are so focused on the ill-being of the organization, customers, clients, staff, coworkers, and the upper echelon that they fail to watch out for their own *Miz-Interests*. For example, there are some who have spent enormous amounts of time and energy developing genuine meaningless organizational policies and equally vague, conflicting procedures that have raised the *Annoyance Factor* to over the nine-point rating. Yet, because they are perceived to be unapproachable, practically everyone else savours and hoards the frustration, while the *Miz-Manager* is left with only a few crumbs of occasional pestering questions. It hardly seems fair. Where is the justice in that?

Elsewhere in this book, a number of *Miz-Management* characteristics will be explored, and the possibilities of why this phenomenon seems to occur so frequently may be examined. Although no conclusions will be offered, along with the description of each characteristic, there may be some useless suggestions and unproven examples of ways to alter these conditions and possibly enrich your own personal *Miz-Experience*.

Once the fundamentals of *Miz-Management* have been vaguely outlined, each fundamental may be dealt with in less detail in subsequent chapters. Originally there were only seven fundamentals, which apparently was purely coincidental with the number of habits of some allegedly highly effective *Brillies*. But then one day, out of the blue, a mysterious eighth habit appeared on bookstore shelves, so in order to preserve the coincidence, an eighth fundamental had to be added.

At the back of this book, you may notice that there are several pages of stickers. There is a sticker for each of the eight behavioural characteristics. Although stickers can have many applications, they have two primary functions in the field of *Miz-Management*. The first is that they can be placed strategically within your employee's workstations to acknowledge that they have mastered the attributes of the specific posted characteristics, similar to badges awarded to Boy Scouts and Girl Guides. Just imagine their *Miz-Gratitude* at being publicly recognized for their achievements and contributions to building an effective *Miz-Environment*. For those employees who prefer to wear their stickers as badges of honour, simply place the sticker in a prominent place on their person, such as their forehead.

The second function is that they can be applied directly to performance appraisals, just like the stars that teachers use in grade school. Although some *Mizzies* really look forward to suffering through the performance appraisal process every year, let's face it, written appraisals rarely achieve their intended objectives. If a picture is worth a thousand words, imagine what can be said with a few graphic stickers. By selecting them appropriately for each employee, there is a greater likelihood of accomplishing the most effective results, without having to write anything. Also, a considerable amount of time can be diverted to more effective *Miz-Use*.

If you were observant enough to have noticed the absence of an index, you may also have spotted that there is both a Chapter III and a Chapter 3. If you haven't already abandoned this book and things like this induce in you a sense of exhilarating annoyance, then you are probably someone who appreciates the *Miz-Genius* in the writers of the Bob Newhart Show, who gave Larry two brothers named Darrel. Chances are you will make an excellent *Miz-Manager*. If, on the other hand, you are having some difficulty accepting that there can be a Chapter III and a Chapter 3 in the same book, then it is quite apparent that you are afflicted with a debilitating *Brillie* condition known as the "Logic Complex." Unfortunately, this means that you lack even a modicum of *Miz-Aptitude,* and it would be most appreciated if you would simply cease reading and return this book from whence it came.

Fortunately, the number of Canadians addicted to logic is extremely low, and the application of common sense is even rarer. If you should find yourself in an organization that has unfortunately been infiltrated by *Brillies,* who bring with them attributes such as intelligence and responsibility, you may be hoping to find some useful examples in this book to counter the *Brillie* impact. Be prepared to enjoy disappointment.

Miz-Management is really about leadership and management style, but the word "Leadership" often conjures up images of pro-action and is commonly associated with decision-making, which may be somewhat disingenuous in the field of *Miz-Management.* Despite the very best intentions of many *Miz-Managers,* sometimes actions or decisions can backfire and even lead to disastrous *Miz-Success* stories. The key to effective *Miz-Management* is to avoid or defer taking any actions or make any decisions at all, thus eliminating any possibility of making any errors in judgement.

Mastering the principles of *Miz-Management* is a sure-fire means of both generating a delightfully frustrating workplace environment and curtailing the ability of any *Brillies* in your organization to undermine your *Miz-Objectives.* Once attained, however, sustaining these objectives are somewhat more challenging. It requires an artful ability to maintain the delicate balance between perception and reality. Avoiding decisions and not taking action is really quite easy, but avoiding the associated accountability or, even better, deflecting the responsibility to someone else is a real art.

While the primary intention of this book is to provide *Miz-Managers* with a minimum of innovative ways to exacerbate their quest for disappointment and enhance their *Miz-Experience,* it is also my sincere hope that it may elicit some warm-hearted annoyance, along with a few fond moments of consternation, nausea, and despair through hours of gratifying tedium. Hopefully, the reckonings of Red Knech included in this book will assist *Miz-Managers* everywhere in finding (and keeping) their own 'Zan,' but that is a most unlikely possibility.

Miz-Enthral!

James

Chapter I

Who the heck is Red Knech?

"It was a cold and windy day in October."

I have no idea why so many books start with a weather report, but a lot of them seem to have been quite successful. So, even though it has nothing to do with anything, I figured that it couldn't hurt, since it really was a cold and windy day in October, as it usually is in Edmonton, which is loosely located somewhere a bit north of the 49th parallel.

I had agreed to take time away from my studies at the University of Alberta to join my family for Thanksgiving dinner at my parent's house. I was still struggling to find a topic for my MBA thesis, and the loss of valuable research time tempted me to find an excuse not to go. But, as usual, guilt outweighed my antipathy for family obligations, and I bowed to the pressure.

The downside of this decision meant that I had to forego my gourmet macaroni and cheese dinner in favour of a simple home cooked turkey dinner with all the trimmings and then swallow my pride by allowing my Dad to discreetly slip a fifty into my pocket while I pretended not to notice. Ah, the sacrifices I make for my family!

On the upside, I always enjoyed the shocked reaction from my aunt Mary at the realization that I was so much taller than when I was five years old. The customary chitchat with aunts and uncles soon guaranteed that everyone was up-to-date on family affairs. Although my Uncle John's apparent incredulity that I was actually attending University was always a bit disconcerting, but after four years of the same questions, over and over, I was finally getting used to it. I could never figure out if he was bewildered that the University had accepted me as a student or surprised that I would actually want to be there.

Small talk with cousins, who have little in common can even be more tedious, but I have to admit, I was genuinely pleased to see my cousin Danny, as he rarely attends family functions. I quite admired him for managing to reach the ripe old age of 24 without yielding to constant parental pressure to advance his education beyond grade twelve. Living on his own for the past five years did not seem to have had any impact on his ability to maintain his gangly appearance. I had mistakenly attributed his trim waist to the exercise that a postman gets by walking several miles each day, but apparently letter sorters don't do that much walking. I soon learned that his lean figure was entirely attributable to his unique diet of personally prepared culinary delights—if you consider BBQ sausages and grilled cheese sandwiches delightful.

After catching up on personal issues, the subject of my thesis dilemma somehow entered the conversation. Danny mentioned that he knew someone, a fellow with the unlikely name of Red Knech (pronounced *neck*), that had a peculiar perspective on the subject of management, which he thought I might find very interesting. He snickered when he told me that this fellow has been working on a book on the subject for at least thirteen years, a book, which no one has ever seen. This made me doubt his ability to provide any viable insights into the complex world of management. However, I was both curious and desperate, so I encouraged Danny to tell me all about his friend.

I soon learned that Red was somewhat uncharacteristic of most Scottish immigrants in that he was highly opinionated, quite outspoken, and his last name 'Knech' did not have a Scottish tartan associated with it. The lack of a tartan was probably due to the fact that his father was from Austria. Apparently, when Red was twelve, his father had a reverie and realized that Scotland and his Scottish wife were incompatible with his desired lifestyle, so he moved to Ireland. Three years later, in defiance of his mother, Red dropped out of school and went to live with his father in Dublin. When he turned eighteen, he left Ireland to join Butlin's Holiday Camp in Clacton-on-Sea as a Red Coat. After wasting nine months there, he immigrated to Canada to continue his education in Newfoundland, where he managed not to complete his BA in less than 3 years. With that failure solidly under his belt, he moved out west and went on to hold a number of insignificant positions with such notable companies as Nortel, Group Action, Bre-X, and JetsGo.

Now in his mid-fifties, Red works as a mail sorter for Canada Post, where he is also a union steward. This means that, although he has a job with the Post Office, he is not seriously expected to do much real work, as this tends to interfere with what he believes to be his union steward obligations. During slow periods at work, which are evidently quite numerous, he spends most of his time writing his reckonings on a variety of subjects. Apparently, the rejection of his numerous submissions by almost every publisher in Canada, the UK, and the USA has done little to discourage him or deter him from sharing his thoughts with anyone willing (or unwilling) to listen.

As Danny was writing down Red's number, he glanced up and grinned at me. "I'm not sure if he'll talk to you or not, but even if he does, you may have difficulty understanding him."

"Why is that?" I asked curiously.

"Partly it's his accent," Danny replied with a devious smile.

"His accent?" I asked curiously, "you mean he still has a Scottish accent?"

"Not exactly," Danny responded slowly, "he sounds more like… Rick Mercer trying to imitate Mike Myers doing his 'Shrek' voice."

"Oh," I murmured, "a Newfy with a bad Scottish/Irish accent then?"

"Something like that. But even if you can get past the accent, you may still have difficulty trying to understand him."

Not knowing exactly what Danny meant by that remark, I somewhat sheepishly accepted the note he handed me and stuffed it into my back pocket, with no intention of ever contacting Mr. Red Knech.

About a week later, I was at my parents place, and my Mom was watching one of her favourite movies '*Gypsy*,' with Rosalind Russell and Natalie Wood. Although it's not on the top of my old movie list, there is one scene that I particularly liked. I arrived just as this scene was starting with the three burlesque ladies showing Natalie their respective gimmicks. As I chuckled at these creative ways of '*bumping*,' it occurred to me that I too needed a gimmick. Suddenly recalling the note with Red Knech's phone number in my back pocket, I realized that, if Danny was right, Red might be just the gimmick I needed. As my desperation increased, my feelings of scepticism were subdued by my curiosity, and I decided to make arrangements to meet with this Mr. Red Knech.

CHAPTER II

RED'S REVELATION

Red Knech and I met for the first time on a Saturday afternoon at a popular Second Cup coffee shop on Whyte Avenue in Edmonton, which, contrary to what some people believe, is not a suburb of Calgary. I brought with me my brand-new leather bound journal that my sister had given to me for my birthday, but I had no idea what it might contain by the end of this meeting.

Upon entering the Second Cup, I scanned the mixed array of customers until I spotted the man I presumed to be my objective. Exactly as he had described himself, Red Knech was sitting at a table in the far corner wearing a checkered shirt and his favourite Guinness baseball cap; it had a bottle opener stitched into the peak.

James Alden: Good afternoon. You must be Mr. Knech.

Red Knech: Aye! That's me.

J :   My name's James Alden. We spoke on the phone?

R :   So that was you then? The one who needs help with a thesis. Good day to y' laddie.

J :   It's a real pleasure to meet you, Mr. Knech.

R :   It's Red, Jimmy.

J :   That's your first name, right?

R :   No, Jimmy, its Ephred, but you can call me Red.

J :   OK. What's the 'F' stand for?

R :   What 'F', Jimmy?

J :   The initial 'F' before Red.

R :   There's no 'F' in Ephred, Jimmy.

J :   I'm confused. Can you spell it out for me?

R :   Aye, Jimmy. E-P-H-R-E-D.

J :   Ephred? So it's one word?

R :   It's not even hyphenated, Jimmy.

J :   So Ephred is your first name?

R :   Is that a problem for y' Jimmy?

J : No. No, it's just…

R : An unusual name, Jimmy?

J : That's it.

R : Is Alfred an unusual name, Jimmy?

J : No, not really.

R : How about Ethelred the Unready, Jimmy?

J : It's not too common today.

R : Well then, Jimmy, are we done with introductions?

J : Uh yeah, we're good.

R : You know Danny then, Jimmy?

J : Oh yeah. Danny's my cousin. I understand he works with you at the Post Office?

R : Aye, Jimmy, Danny's a good lad, but somewhat confused. I suppose it's a family trait with you and your cousin then is it?

J : Danny did warn me about confusion. Anyway, as I mentioned on the phone, I'm doing some research for my thesis on Management Theories, and Danny gave me your name as someone who has a particularly unique perspective on this subject.

R : Possibly, Jimmy.

J : Umm… can I get you a coffee or something, Mr. Knech?

R : Don't mind if I do. I'll have a large, extra hot, light on the foam, double maple, skim milk latte, with a shot of vanilla, caramel topping and cinnamon sprinkles. Oh, and a Cranberry Peach muffin, as you're offering.

J : Right then…
(returning with coffees)
Here we are… one whatever it was you ordered. Hope I got it right. Sorry it took so long, but the line was slow.

R : Not a problem, Jimmy. Most appreciated.

J : First I'd like to thank you for agreeing to this interview on such short notice.

R : Not at all, Jimmy.

J : Before we get started, I have a couple of questions that need clarification… just for the record, you understand.

R : Right, Jimmy. Are you going to write it all down in that leather book then?

J : That's the plan if you have no objections.

R : Not as long as you get it down correctly, Jimmy.

J : That's great, Mr. Knech.

R : It's Red, Jimmy.

J : OK, right, Red it is. Is Red short for Ephred?

R : No, Jimmy. I borrowed it from Red Green.

J : That's a great show. I really enjoy Red Green.

R : Me too, Jimmy, now maybe we should get started then.

J : OK, we could start with the proper spelling of your last name?

R : It's Knech, Jimmy, 'K-N-E-C-H'. Although the 'K' is silent, the 'CH' is pronounced like a 'K'.

J : OK. Got it. And I already know that Ephred is your real first name?

R : Red is real to me, Jimmy.

J : Well, is that the name on your driver's license?

R : I don't have a driver's license, Jimmy.

J : What's on your birth certificate?

R : Oh? You want that name then, Jimmy? It's Kneil Kenneth Knech.

J : Not Ephred?

R : No, Jimmy.

J : Is that Neill with one 'L' or two?

R : One, Jimmy, and a 'K.'

J : There's a 'K' in Neil?

R : There is if you spell it 'K-N-E-I-L', Jimmy. My mother liked the name Neil, but she was obsessed with the letter 'K', which is why she married m' Da.'

J : Because his name started with a 'K?'

R : Aye, Jimmy.

J : Do you think that's a good enough reason to get married?

R : Well if it isn't, Jimmy, I wouldn't be here.

J : I see your point. So your initials are actually KKK, is that right?

R : No, Jimmy.

J : No?

R : They're just E.K.

J : But I thought you said it was Kneil Kenneth Knech?

R : You asked what was on my birth certificate Jimmy, but I had it legally changed when I was eighteen.

J : So… you didn't like KKK for initials?

R : I'm not into wearing sheets, Jimmy.

J : Not exactly Canada Post issue I suppose. So why did you pick the name Ephred?

R : I didn't, Jimmy. My mother picked it for me as part of the deal.

J : What deal was that?

R : Well Jimmy, she didn't really want me to change m'name, but she wouldn't be too upset if I took the name of my great to the 18th power grandfather…

J : Which was Ephred?

R : No, Jimmy, it was Ethelred.

J : So how did it get to be Ephred then?

R : She can't spell, Jimmy.

J : OK then, 'Red' is now your name, right?

R : Aye, Jimmy.

J : Good! Well, not to change the subject, but do I detect a slight Scottish accent?

R : Good ear laddie, but just for the record, it's not me with the accent, Jimmy, it's you. The Scots were speaking the language of Robbie Burns long before this country was even invented.

J : Point taken.

R : Although I don't speak it as well as I used to, Jimmy. After living on the Emerald Isle for a few years, then England and now here in Canada, m' speech has become a bit contaminated.

J : You lived in Ireland for a few years then?

R : Did I not just say that, Laddie?

J : Right. So, after Ireland, you moved to Newfoundland?

R : No, Jimmy, I lived in England for a wee while before coming over here.

J : But I understand that you spent some time in Newfoundland before coming out west.

R : Aye, Jimmy

J : It's James.

R : What is, Jimmy?

J : My name, it's James.

R : I know that, Jimmy. You told me that already. Is there a reason that you're telling me again then, Jimmy?

J : Apparently not!

R : Y'know what's interesting, Jimmy? The good folks in Newfoundland don't seem to have the strong accent that you Albertans have.

J : Well, as long as we can understand each other, does it matter?

R : Not really, Jimmy, but accents can cause confusion.

J : OK… then, moving along… do you really have some kind of new theory on management behaviour?

R : Reckonings, Jimmy.

J : Reckonings?

R : Aye, Jimmy. It's not really a theory; it's just my personal reckonings.

J : OK. Do you have some interesting reckonings on management?

R : I do, Jimmy.
(Pause)

J : Uh good… could you explain them to me?

R : I'd be happy to.
(Pause)

J : When?

R : As soon as you ask me, Jimmy? As I recall, you told me on the phone that you'd ask the questions and all I'd have to do was answer. Did I misunderstand something then?

J : No, not at all. That is what we agreed to. So, Red, could you please tell me a bit about your reckonings?

R : Delighted to, Jimmy. As you can see by the white hair, I've been around for a while, and I've had 162 different jobs—actually 163, if I count the one and a half hours I worked for McDonald's in Cornerbrook, Newfoundland.

J : You had a job that lasted for only one-and-a-half hours?

R : Aye, I did, Jimmy.

J : When was this?

R : Between 6 and 7:30 in the morning, Jimmy.

J : No, I meant, what year?

R : Oh, it was a long time ago, Jimmy.

J : What happened?

R : It was because of the broken eggs then, Jimmy.

J : Broken eggs? Don't you have to break a few
eggs to make an egg McMuffin?

R : True, Jimmy, but not all of them.

J : All? Exactly how many did you break?

R : About 18 or 19.

J : That's all?

R : Dozen!

J : Oh!

R : But the manager was really good about it, Jimmy. He was quite
concerned for my future. He strongly suggested that it might
be in my best interest to consider a different vocation and then
he gave me two hours pay before he showed me the door.

J : OK well, that was very interesting, but maybe we could get back to your reckonings?

R : Right. Well you see, Jimmy, I've worked for a lot of different types of managers. When I was much younger, I assumed that they were all either idiots or just plain stupid.

J : I suppose if you've worked for 162 different managers,
you're bound to encounter a few that aren't perfect.

R : More than a just few, Jimmy. So, I asked myself, *how can there be so
many incompetent managers out there? Can they all really be that obtuse?*

J : Obtuse?

R : Not at all, Jimmy, I'm sharp as a tack.

J : Of course.

R : Back then, I reckoned that it was just their confused thinking and sometimes even bad luck that generated so much
incompetence. Or perhaps it was the Peter Principle at
work, as proposed in Dr. Laurence J. Peter's book.

J : Is that the one that states "in a hierarchy, every employee tends to rise to his level of incompetence?"

R : I see you know the Peter Principle then, Jimmy.

J : Doesn't everyone? It's a classic.

R : It's also still relevant today, Jimmy. And for a while, I thought maybe these folks were mostly just P^3s (pronounced - *P threes*).

J : P^3s? You mean like the Public Private Partnership type of P^3s?

R : No, Jimmy. P^3 is an inappropriate name for those
types of P^3s. They should really be called P4s.

J : P4s? Why's that?

R : Public Private Profiteering Partnership, Jimmy.

J : Sounds like you aren't a big fan of these types of arrangements.

R : No, I really like them, Jimmy. They are champions of mediocrity, and they clearly support my reckonings on *Miz-Management*.

J : I hate to break this to you Red, but P4s are already taken.

R : Really, Jimmy?

J : P4s are high containment laboratories in Europe, similar to our Bio-Safety Level 4 laboratory in Winnipeg for highly contagious human and animal pathogens and viruses.

R : Now who's speaking gibberish, Jimmy? And where did you learn that curious bit of information.

J : I got it out of a biology lab assignment by completing a research paper on high containment labs.

R : Why was that, Jimmy?

J : I just hated lab work and this was an optional assignment.

R : So Jimmy, your undergrad degree was in Science, was it?

J : How did you guess?

R : Intuition, Jimmy.

J : OK, so we know what P4s are what are P^3s?

R : Peter Principle People, Jimmy.

J : Are these P^3s a key component of your reckonings?

R : Not exactly, Jimmy, but they are the masochist's most important allies.

J : Masochists?

R : Didn't I just say that, Jimmy?

J : That is what I heard, but what do masochists have to do with your reckonings on management behaviour?

R : Everything, Jimmy. It came to me like an astonishing revelation.

J : Like in a dream?

R : Not exactly, Jimmy, it was daytime. Y'see Jimmy, I was attending this management conference somewhere, and as was m'custom, I was just starting to nod off when something woke me with a start. As I slowly looked around, I noticed, as if for the very first time, that the room was dark and dreary, the chairs were utterly painful, and the speaker was dryer than Nevada.

J : Sounds like a typical conference.

R : It was bloody miserable, Jimmy. But more importantly, I realized that everyone else in the room must be equally miserable, and it occurred to me that most of them had paid good money to be there.

J : Most? Including you?

R : Don't be daft, Jimmy. I never pay to go to a conference. If I can't get someone else to pay, then I don't go.

J : OK, can we get back to your revelation?

R : Well Jimmy, I had an epiphanic moment, when it was revealed to me that many seemingly irrational management decisions were not a result of P^3 incompetence but were actually purposeful.

J : What purpose is that?

R : Misery, Jimmy.

J : I'm confused again.

R :   That seems to happen to you a lot, Jimmy. You
         might want to see someone about it.

J :   Or… I could just leave.

R :   But will it make you miserable, Jimmy?

J :   Do I want to be miserable?

R :   You would if you were a masochist, Jimmy.

J :   Well, I'm not.

R :   Maybe not, Jimmy, but let's pretend you are.
         What would your decision be?

J :   I suppose, I'd just stay here and get more confused.

R :   There you have it, Jimmy. While others may see that as an ir-
         rational decision, it makes sense to a masochist.

J :   So what exactly are you saying, Red?

R :   Just this, Jimmy; masochists make deliberate decisions that gen-
         erate misery for themselves and others around them.

J :   Are you saying that some management decisions that ap-
         pear on the surface to be a result of P^3 incompetence are, in
         fact, deliberately bad decisions made by masochists?

R :   Not at all, Jimmy; they're well meaning deci-
         sions, with the intention to create misery.

J :   So what do P^3s and masochists have in common?

R :   Good question, Jimmy. P^3s are Managers who have been el-
         evated to their level of incompetence, and masochists are man-
         agers who are just perceived as being incompetent.

J :   How do you tell the difference?

R :   That's a tough one, Jimmy. P^3s make poor decisions be-
         cause they don't know what they are doing, and masoch-
         ists make decisions that are deliberate but perceived as be-
         ing poor because they are attempting to create misery.

J :   So these are really good decisions that look like bad decisions.

R :   No, Jimmy, they're not really good.

J :   I'm confused again. Didn't you just say they were really good?

R :   Well meaning, Jimmy, but not really good. That's the problem.

J :   What's the problem?

R :   Y'see Jimmy, masochists need to learn how to make re-
         ally good decisions, not just mediocre decisions.

J :   It still sounds like incompetence.

R :   Well Jimmy, it can be confusing to the uninitiated.

J :   Like me?

R :   To put it in simple terms, Jimmy, P^3s are incompetent manag-
         ers who are delusional in thinking they are doing a good job and
         believe they are actually making their units run effectively.

J :   But they aren't effective, is that right?

R :   Aye, Jimmy. Masochist managers, on the other hand, are deliber-
         ately attempting to undermine the effectiveness of the organization

with the object of creating a miserable working environment.

J : So let me see if I got this right; P³s are incompetent managers who screw up unintentionally, and masochists are incompetent managers who screw up deliberately but need to learn how to screw up even more to create a really miserable working environment?

R : Not quite, Jimmy. It's true that P³s are incompetent and therefore ineffective because they don't know any better. Masochists, however, are actually not incompetent. Their behaviour is only perceived as being ineffective because they are trying to intentionally be miserable.

J : But do they really need to learn how to do it better?

R : They do, Jimmy. When it became apparent to me that many of the intended objectives of masochists were not being successfully achieved, I knew they needed help.

J : Were they having problems with knowing how to create misery, or were they being thwarted in their efforts by people who actually knew what they were doing?

R : Both, Jimmy. It was clear to me that these people were neither imbeciles nor obtuse. They were just masochists.

J : Masochists who need your help?

R : Exactly, Jimmy. I mean there must be a million books out there on management, and some of them are even quite good, but are there any for masochists? No!

J : There's a surprise. So did you follow up on your revelations with any studies to support your reckonings?

R : Well Jimmy I wish I could say that it was it was my astute powers of observation of the abnormally high frequency and constant repetition of this ubiquitous behaviour that brought me to enlightenment, but that's not very believable, and it sounds a bit pretentious.

J : Perhaps just a bit, but at least you achieved enlightenment?

R : Not the kind you mean, Jimmy. But I did do some research, starting with the Oxford Dictionary, which defines masochism as 'a form of perversion characterized by gratification derived from one's own pain or humiliation, or the enjoyment of what appears to be painful or tiresome.'

J : I know what a masochist is.

R : Fair enough, Jimmy, but not everyone knows that the word is named after the Austrian novelist L. von Sacher-Masoch.

J : Perhaps not, but is that important?

R : Not really, Jimmy, but as my father was Austrian, I've always been a bit curious about what other unusual characters Austria has produced.

J : I didn't think von Sacher-Masoch was, himself, a masochist. I thought he just defined the condition.

R : True, Jimmy, but Austria seems to have produced more than its share, which might explain why a highly successful Austrian movie star would give up an enviable and lucrative movie career in favour of politics and then cheat on his wife, knowing that he'd eventually get caught.

J : Lots of people are attracted to politics.

R : Mostly masochists, Jimmy.

J : That's ridiculous.

R : Not really, Jimmy. This is a good example of a masochist who just came out of the closet.

J : The closet? Are you're saying that they are gay?

R : Don't be daft, Jimmy. They're closet masochists.

J : Closet masochists?

R : I just said that, Jimmy. The problem is that the vast majority of masochists continue to remain in the closet, partly because being a masochist is not generally considered to be socially acceptable, but also because they don't really like the term 'masochist'.

J : Really? I wonder why?

R : Most seem to prefer to be called '*Mizzies*'

J : 'Mizzies,' not masochists—really?

R : True, Jimmy. I think you're getting the picture.

J : I think the picture I'm getting is a refill. More coffee, Red?

R : No thanks, Jimmy. Too much caffeine is not good for you.

J : Good point. I'm also a bit *Mizzed-Out*.

R : And what is that supposed to mean, Jimmy?

J : Nothing Red. But we've covered a lot of ground today, and as much as I'd love to delve into the details, I do have another commitment, so we'll have to continue this discussion another time.

R : When, Jimmy?

J : When?

R : Aye when, Jimmy?

J : Well—

R : I'm available tomorrow.

J : Uh well, OK, I suppose.

R : Right Jimmy, see y'here at two o'clock.

Red quickly rose from his seat, patted me softly on the back, and headed out the door. I sat there in a daze, still reeling from the effects of this bizarre conversation. The logical side of my brain was annoyed that I couldn't say no to tomorrow's session, and the curious side was contemplating the possibilities. Could there actually be some useful thesis material here, or was it all just gibberish?

I closed my leather journal, leaned back in my chair, and exhaled softly. The last time I experienced this type of exhaustion was two years ago, during a one-week French immersion excursion to Quebec City. We were not allowed to speak any English for the entire week, and as beneficial as that experience was, it was also mentally draining. I felt like I had just spent an hour with someone who speaks a foreign language.

I glanced down at my journal, but I could not find the energy to even re-open it. It had crossed my mind more than once that maybe Danny had really set me up. I imagined him sitting in a bar somewhere waiting for Red, or whatever his real name was, to join him for a few beers and have a good laugh at my expense. Now I felt like a real idiot and decided it was time to go home.

Chapter III

Mizzies, Brillies and Sleepers

When I woke up on Sunday morning, I felt great. The thought of Red Knech was furthest from my mind as I stepped into the shower, and I was looking forward to a relaxing Sunday. Unfortunately, the warmth of the shower seemed to unlock the repressed memory of my close encounter of the weird kind, and suddenly I was shivering at the very thought of another session with the portentous Mr. Red Knech.

I spent the rest of the morning concocting excuses that could get me out of my scheduled meeting with Red. When I finally settled on a good one, I picked up the phone and made the call. There was no answer—and no answering machine.

Now what? I considered just not showing up, but somehow I couldn't do that. After wrestling with my conscience for some time, I reluctantly decided to honour my commitment, hoping against hope that he would fail to show.

Unfortunately, when I arrived ten minutes late, Red was seated at the same table, intently perusing the Edmonton Sun.

J :   Good afternoon, Red. How are you today?

R :   Great, Jimmy. I was wondering if you'd changed your mind.

J :   Sorry I'm late; I see you don't have a coffee or anything.

R :   Very observant, Jimmy. I was waiting for you.

J :   What'll you have then?

R :   Same as yesterday, Jimmy, if you don't mind?

J :   I'm not sure I can remember exactly what that was.

R :   It's all in your leather notebook there, Jimmy. I noticed you wrote everything down.

J :   Of course, I'll be right back.

R :   Great, Jimmy.

J :   OK, here it is. I hope I got it right.

R :   Thanks very much, Jimmy.

J :   So Red, you were saying that some people, particularly managers, who are masochists, prefer to be called *Mizzies*?

R :   Right, Jimmy, but the problem is that most of them are closet *Mizzies,* and they have trouble being open about their real feelings and objectives.

J :   Meaning that most of them don't use or even know about the term *Mizzy,* is that right?

R :   You are quicker than you look, Jimmy. Now I have noticed that some women have adopted the term 'Ms.' which is pronounced the same as *Miz,* 'M-I-Z' and there are a few miserable 'geeks' who call themselves *Miz-Kids,* but that doesn't necessarily mean they are *Mizzies.* They are more like *Mizzy*-Wanna-bees.

J :   Fascinating reckoning, Red. Do you have a name for what we are talking about?

R :   It's really quite simple, Jimmy. It's called *Miz-Management.*

J :   Miz-Management?

R :   I just said that, Jimmy. You're probably familiar with the works of Victor Hugo and his masterpiece 'Les Miserables' and the world famous musical of the same name, based on Hugo's novel.

J :   I think most people are familiar with Les Miserables.

R :   Well Jimmy, as you know, Les Miserables has become affectionately known as 'Les Miz.' Since *Miz* is a contraction of the word miserable, *Miz-Management* simply means miserable management.

J :   Really? Do you think that *Miz-Management* is a growing trend in the management field?

R :   It's always been there, Jimmy. But as we discussed, *Miz-Management* is not to be confused with poor management or incompetent P^3 management. It's more analogous to a particular philosophical approach to management where a state of misery is the primary objective behind all key management decisions.

J :   You're not actually serious about this, are you?

R :   I'm dead serious, Jimmy, and I've done all the research to prove it.

J :   Will that be in the book that you're working on?

R :   It would indeed, Jimmy, if I could get around to it, but it's a slow process.

J :   How far are you with this book?

R :   Well Jimmy, I have a name for it.

J :   And that would be?

R :   I call it "Zan and the Mythical Art of Miz-Management."

J :   Did you say "Zan?"

R :   That's right, Jimmy.

J :   Don't you mean "Zen?"

R :   No. It's definitely Zan—nothing to do with Zen at all.

J :   So what is Zan?

R :   Actually, Jimmy, it's a nickname for Alexandra.

J :   Who's that?

R :   My first wife, Jimmy. Although I didn't really appreciate it at the time, life with Zan was a euphoric state of misery.

J :   So it wasn't a great marriage then?

R : No it was incredible, Jimmy. I would probably still be with her today, had I not foolishly lost my temper and thunderously berated her boyfriend.

J : Your wife's boyfriend?

R : You know Jimmy, the damage could have easily been repaired with a simple grovelling apology, but I was young and impetuous, and before I knew it, life with Zan was over.

J : What happened?

R : Off she went, Jimmy, on the back of his motorcycle, never to be seen again.

J : She left you?

R : Me and Canada, Jimmy. You know it's true what they say, *you never appreciate what you have until it's gone.*

J : Very true!

R : The point is, Jimmy, that every *Mizzy* needs their own personal '*Zan*' to bring meaningful and constant misery into their lives. What I'm hoping is that the insights included in this book will be able to assist *Mizzies* everywhere to find and to keep their own 'Zan.'

J : Do you seriously think there's a market for a book on *Miz-Management*?

R : Aye Jimmy, it's huge, HUGE. They need this book so they don't make so many *Miz-Takes*.

J : What kind of mistakes?

R : I said *Miz-Takes,* Jimmy; not quite the same thing.

J : How so?

R : A mistake is an error due to incompetence, Jimmy, like our P^3 managers. But a *Miz-Take* is an error due to inexperience.

J : Isn't that the same thing?

R : No Jimmy, the difference between incompetence and inexperience is that inexperience is curable.

J : And you have discovered the cure, is that it?

R : Maybe, Jimmy.

J : So how much research have you've completed on *Miz-Management*?

R : No need, Jimmy, just look around.

J : You mean here in Second Cup?

R : Not exactly, Jimmy. But looking around, I expect there are more *Brillies* in here than *Mizzies*.

J : Brillies?

R : Aye, *Brillies*. Y'see Jimmy, that's what *Mizzies* call *Non-Mizzies,* who are not P^3s.

J : What does that mean?

R : It means they are not incompetent, Jimmy.

J : And how did you come up with that name?

R : It's brilliant, Jimmy.

J : Maybe it is brilliant, but I still don't get it?

R : It's simply brilliant, Jimmy, that's all!

J : What's so brilliant about it?

R : Nothing, Jimmy… it's just a contraction of the word 'brilliant.'

J : So, all *Non-Mizzies* are brilliant, is that it?

R : Not at all, Jimmy. P³s are never brilliant, but some *Sleepers* are.

J : I don't suppose you have a dictionary with a special *'Red Knech'* vocabulary section?

R : No need, Jimmy, it's dead simple.

J : May be simple to you, Red, but I've never heard of *Mizzies* or *Brillies,* and I don't really understand what you mean by *Sleepers.*

R : Y'see Jimmy, to start with, neither *Brillies* nor *Sleepers* are *Mizzies.*

J : Great. Now we know what they aren't. What are they?

R : Well Jimmy, a *Miz-Manager* comes up with a suggestion—

J : Miz-Manager?

R : Please Jimmy, don't keep repeating me. Now, a *Miz-Manager* is just a Manager who's a *Mizzy*—

J : Ah, right.

R : So, as I was saying, Jimmy, whenever a *Miz-Manager* comes up with a suggestion or a new idea, there's always some sarcastic bastard muttering *'brilliant'* under his breath or in the background somewhere.

J : But they don't mean brilliant; they really mean stupid, don't they?

R : Exactly, Jimmy. You've probably heard this many times.

J : Actually I have, which is a bit worrisome.

R : Isn't it just, Jimmy? Knowing that there's so much sarcasm around.

J : No, that's not what's worrisome. What's worrying to me, is that I'm still listening to you.

R : Well keep listening, Jimmy, or you'll never learn anything.

J : My listening is fine. I'm just having a bit of difficulty following the perverse logic in your reckonings.

R : Could be you're not used to hearing English spoken properly then, Jimmy?

J : Right, that's probably it.

R : Good, Jimmy. Y'see, the fundamentals of *Miz-Management* begin with the assumption that, unlike *Brillies*, *Mizzies* have a desperate need to find a profound state of mental anguish in their lives called the *Miz-State.*

J : Miz-State? Oh good, another new word.

R : No repeats, Jimmy. So to reach that state, they require an environment that provides them with a consistently high level of misery and humiliation. This is called the *Miz-Environment.*

J : Right. Yet another new word!

R : Aye Jimmy, and every *Mizzy* needs this *Miz-Environment* to derive any sense of *Miz-Gratification* and to be able to truly benefit from a *Miz-Experience.*

J : Miz-Experience and Miz—

R : If you're going to repeat everything, Jimmy, we'll be here all day.

J : I really think I need a *'Red Knech – English'* dictionary.

R : Brilliant idea, Jimmy. We'll put it at the end of our book.

J : Our book?

R : There y'go repeating everything again. It's what we've
   been talking about all along, Jimmy. I help you with
   your thesis, and you help me with m'book.
J : Ah... I don't recall that—
R : C'mon now Jimmy, your thesis and my book are practically
   the same, and clearly you're a much better writer, so—
J : So I do all the writing and—
R : I do all the thinking, Jimmy. You get a fancy piece of paper to
   put up on your wall and I get a diminutive amount of money
   from the sale of both copies of the book. Fair enough?
J : Perhaps we should take some time to think about this?
R : What is there to think about? We could have the
   first book wrapped up in just a few weeks.
J : The first book? How many books are we talking about?
R : Eight, but they're just short books, Jimmy.
J : Time for another refill.

Red and I returned to the counter to refresh our coffees. I was a bit worried about having another cup because too much coffee gives me the jitters. As we stood in line, it occurred to me that the act of freshening up one's coffee is kind of like taking a break from a coffee break. With that thought, I realized that Red's logic was actually beginning to intrigue me, just as it seems to have fascinated my cousin Danny. This caused me to wonder if there was any history of mental illness in our family that our grandparents had withheld from us.

J : So, Red, before we go on with your eight books, could
   you go back and explain *Sleepers*? With all the other new words, I seem to have missed that one.
R : No problem, Jimmy. *Sleepers* are actually *Brillies* who
   don't follow the Peter Principle and become P^{3}s, and
   they are the most dangerous types of *Brillies*.
J : Why is that?
R : Well Jimmy, for some strange reason, they seem to know
   where their level of incompetence is, and they chose not to
   go there. They have this curious attraction to a work/life balance condition, so they remain in their comfort zone.
J : Why do think that is?
R : The way I see it, Jimmy, is that most *Sleepers* are usually quite intelligent and they really detest incompetence, both in themselves and
   in other P^3 Managers. They don't believe that prestige is important,
   and many reach a high enough level in the hierarchy that they don't
   seem to need the extra money. So they stay either at, or even below,
   their level of competence, which makes them especially dangerous.
J : Why's that?
R : Well Jimmy, because they are competent, they usually get their
   work done efficiently and effectively, and then they have ex-

tra time to observe the activities of the P^3s around them.

J : And that makes them dangerous?

R : Only if someone wakes them up, Jimmy. If their world is disrupted by a P^3, whoever that may be, a *Sleeper* may awake and expose the P^3 for their incompetence.

J : Do we really care about the P^3s?

R : Absolutely, Jimmy. They are important allies for *Mizzies,* and they have to be protected.

J : From what?

R : From themselves, Jimmy.

J : Of course.

R : But more importantly, Jimmy, *Sleepers* can occasionally thwart the plans of *Miz-Managers.*

J : That sounds real bad.

R : It can be, Jimmy, but fortunately, they are anomalies in the hierarchy, and there aren't that many of them around.

J : Good to know.

R : Aye Jimmy, and the other good thing is that they tend to mind their own business, which is why they are called *Sleepers.*

J : I thought maybe they were like the spies that Russia planted in the US a number of years ago.

R : What spies are y'talking about, Jimmy?

J : Like in the movie 'Salt.'

R : There's a movie about salt, Jimmy?

J : You know, the one with Angelina Jolie?

R : You watch a lot of movies then, do y'Jimmy?

J : Well, I enjoy going to the movies, especially ones with a VIP lounge.

R : What's that then, Jimmy?

J : You know, like the one at the new Cineplex in Windermere?

R : Don't know where that is, Jimmy.

J : It's just across the street from Cabelas.

R : Do you mean the hunting store, Jimmy, with all those guns?

J : That's the one.

R : Haven't been back since they opened, Jimmy.

J : Well the next time you go—

R : Can't go back, Jimmy.

J : Why not?

R : I don't have a truck.

J : You don't need a truck, unless you're buying something big.

R : Y'don't understand, Jimmy, my old Chevette has an inferiority complex, and it won't start when it's surrounded by pickup trucks.

J : You have a Chevette that's still working?

R : Aye Jimmy, unless it's sandwiched between a couple of intimidating pickup trucks. Now, what's this movie about salt then?

J : Never mind.

R : Anyway Jimmy, the point is, it's best not to wake them up.

J : Good plan. Now getting back to the eight books, how did you determine that there should be eight books, and what is each book about?

R : Hold on there, Jimmy, one question at a time.

J : OK, let's focus on the eight books.

R : Well Jimmy, at first it was just seven books. My thinking was that
if seven habits were good enough for a famous author like Mr.
Stephen Covey, then seven should be good enough for me. But
low and behold, one day, an eighth habit suddenly showed up at
bookstores, so naturally I had to reconsider my approach.

J : Naturally!

R : After all Jimmy, Santa has eight reindeer, and Snow White has
eight dwarfs, so eight must also be a good number, right?

J : Snow White only had seven dwarfs.

R : She did, Jimmy, but that's only because Thorin was
driven into exile by the Dragon Smaug.

J : Thorin, from the Lord of the Rings?

R : I'm surprised you didn't know that, Jimmy. He's the one
who hired Bilbo Baggins to steal back the treasure.

J : I must have missed that book. So, are you saying that
Mizzies have eight types of particular habits?

R : No, not at all, Jimmy. It's coincidental with the I Ching.

J : The 'I Ching'?

R : Aye, Jimmy!

J : What's the I Ching, and what does it have to do the eight books?

R : Well y'see Jimmy, the I Ching, which is sometimes called the Book of
Changes, is an ancient Chinese masterpiece that reveals the mysteries of
the universe and can predict the future if you know how to interpret it.

J : And you know how to interpret this ancient book?

R : Haven't got a clue, Jimmy, but it does have eight trigrams,
which is why I chose it, and since no one else really under-
stands it; who's to say that my interpretation is wrong?

J : You can't just arbitrarily link your reckonings to an ancient philosophy without years of study and analysis.

R : Don't be daft, Jimmy! These are my reckonings, and it's not
like there's any copyright infringement here. Whoever wrote
the I Ching has been dead for thousands of years.

J : Is there any real correlation at all between
your reckonings and this *I Ching*?

R : Not that it really matters, Jimmy, but occasionally there seems to be, if
one looks at it in the right perspective. For each of the sixty-four hexagrams in the I Ching, there is a corresponding behavioural characteristic,
which any *Mizzy* can learn to emulate to improve their *Miz-Environment*.

J : I thought you said there were eight numbers.

R : That's right, Jimmy, eight trigrams and sixty-four hexagrams, which make up the eight *Miz-Behavioural* types in each of the eight books.

J :   You mean there are eight groups of eight habits—

R :   No, Jimmy, not habits, *behavioural characteristics*.

J :   As usual, you've lost me again.

R :   No matter, Jimmy, just leave the thinking to me,
and it'll all make sense in due course.

J :   I can hardly wait. Perhaps we could get back to the eight books.

R :   Not now, Jimmy. I just noticed the time, and I have to be on my way.

J :   OK…

R :   I'm off on Tuesday, Jimmy. Meet me at the Second Cup on
the lower level of Telus Plaza at 2 o'clock. See y' then.

I seemed to feel a sense of relief each time Red departed so quickly. However, after this session, I was having some serious doubts about Mr. Knech and his bizarre reckonings. I couldn't see anyway that this material could be adapted into a thesis that would be acceptable to my thesis advisor, and time was running out. The thought of wasting more valuable time with Red again on Tuesday turned my mind to scheming, hoping to figure out some way of avoiding our next session.

CHAPTER IV

THE EIGHT BOOKS OF MIZ

Tuesday afternoon arrived too quickly for me to come up with a good excuse for not meeting with Red, so I quickly began reviewing my notes. I couldn't find much hope of uncovering any thesis material in all this mess, but still having no other alternative thesis concept, desperation assailed me, so here I was again trekking to the Second Cup at Telus Plaza, devoid of any haste or enthusiasm. Red was anxiously waiting, like a spider waiting for a fly. Maybe I really was a closet Mizzie.

THE EIGHT BOOKS OF MIZ

☰ Book I - Ch'ien
MIZ-GUIDING PRINCIPALS AND
MIZ-LEADING PROTOCOLS WITHOUT MORELS

☷ Book II - K'un
TURKEY SOUP FOR THE MIZ-FORTUNATE SOLE

☳ Book III - Chen
ZAN AND THE MYTHICAL ART OF MIZ-MANAGEMENT

☵ Book IV - K'an
MIZ-ADVENTURES ON THE ROAD LES TRAVELLED

☶ Book V - Ken
THE JOEY OF MIZ-BEHAVING

☴ Book VI - Sun
MIZ-UNDERSTANDING AND LEARNING
THE IMPORTANCE OF CHANGE

☲ Book VII - Li
MIZ-FITNESS FOR SMARTIES

☱ Book VIII - Tui
THE ONE HABIT OF HOLY SUCCESSFUL
MIZ-BELIEVERS

J : Afternoon, Red. Coffee?

R : Please, Jimmy.

J : Here you go, Red, fresh coffee and a muffin.

R : Thanks, Jimmy.

J : So you mentioned the eight miz-behavioural types in each of the eight books.

R : Right, Jimmy. Well, I've already explained a bit about the first one we'll be working on, titled *Zan and the Mythical Art of Miz-Management*.

J : So Zan and the Mythical Art of Miz-Management is Book I?

R : No, Jimmy, it's Book III.

J : But you just said it was the first book?

R : It will be the first book released, Jimmy, but it's Book number III.

J : I suppose you have some curious logic for starting with Book III?

R : It worked for Star Wars, didn't it?

J : I should have seen that coming. At the risk of asking another dumb question, what about the other seven books?

R : There are no dumb questions here, Jimmy, just ignorance that needs to be cured.

J : Why do I get the feeling that the cure is worse than the problem?

R : Must be your suspicious mind, Jimmy.

J : Right. So what about the other seven books?

R : Way ahead of you, Jimmy. Here, I've written them all out for you.

J : How long ago did you write this?

R : Yesterday, Jimmy, why?

J : Well, the writing is starting to fade.

R : It's just the pencil, Jimmy.

J : But the paper is yellow!

R : Aye, Jimmy, with light blue lines.

J : So you wrote it with a soft pencil on crumpled yellow paper?

R : C'mon Jimmy, it's not that crumpled. It's just a wee bit folded here and there.

J : But why on yellow lined notepaper?

R : That's what the Canada Post keeps in stock, Jimmy.

J : Oh, I see. It's the Post Office's fault. It's really difficult to read on this yellow paper.

R : That's because you've smudged the pencil, Jimmy.

J : No, I think it's pre-smudged.

R : It's crystal clear, Jimmy! Quite legible to any postal worker.

J : Of course.

R : Y'see Jimmy, it has each of the eight book titles neatly written out and numbered from one to eight.

J : So if I'm reading this correctly, Book I is called *Ch'ien* in Chinese?

R : Right on, Jimmy, see how easy it is to read?

J : Which translates into Red Knechian as, Miz-Guiding Principals and Miz-Leading Protocols, without Morels? Is that right?

R : Maybe not exactly, Jimmy, but I'm sure it's close enough.

J : OK then, what exactly does Ch'ien mean?

R : Well Jimmy, as near as I can figure, it means either *'Father'* or *'Heaven'.*

J : Which somehow correlates with your title for Book I?

R : Use your imagination, Jimmy.

J : I think you might have misspelled "*Principles*" and "*Morals.*"

R : Why is that then, Jimmy?

J : Well, a Principal means a main thing or a head person, such as the principal of a school and—

R : Exactly right, Jimmy.

J : You're saying that's what you mean?

R : Correct again, Jimmy.

J : It's just that… by the way it's worded… I naturally assumed that you were referring to fundamental principles or a personal code of conduct such as moral principles or something.

R : Well then, Jimmy, you'd be wrong.

J : I see. Would I also be assuming incorrectly if I suggested that you misspelled the word *morals?*

R : Why would you think that, Jimmy?

J : Because when you spell morals with an 'e' instead of an 'a' it means a type of mushroom or edible fungus.

R : You really are smarter than you look, Jimmy. You certainly know your words there, laddie. I'll gi'you that. Maybe we could enter you in a Spelling Bee contest.

J : I'm sure I'm going to regret this, but would it be asking too much for a little explanation of the meaning of *Miz-Guiding Principals and Miz-Leading Protocols, without Morels.*

R : Not at all, Jimmy. It's a guide for *Mizzies* to help them to be more effective as *Miz-Leaders* in business and politics. It's all about *Miz-Leadership* and power, Jimmy. *'Father'* represents leadership and *'Heaven'* represents power.

J : Makes no sense at all to me. How does that relate to the title?

R : The title is self-explanatory, Jimmy.

J : Maybe to you, Red, but I'm just an ignorant university student, and I need a little help here. Perhaps you could break it down into smaller pieces, starting with *Miz-Guiding Principals?*

R : It means exactly what it says, Jimmy. Advice garnered from a number of different principals, to serve as a guide for *Miz-Leaders* in politics and business.

J : Are you saying that these principals are people, like school principals?

R : Well some may be, Jimmy, but most are principals in consulting firms.

J : You mean *principal*, as in partners in a business firm?

R : Exactly, Jimmy. Industry *Miz-Leaders.*

J : And Miz-Leading Protocols?

R : Surely you know what a protocol is, Jimmy?

J : Of course, *rules of behaviour, usually in a formal context.*

R : Aye, so what's your question then, Jimmy?

J : Perhaps you could give me an example of a *Miz-Leading* Protocol?

R : There'll be examples in the book, Jimmy, if we ever get to it.

J : OK, fine, but what do you mean by *without Morels?*

R : That's dead obvious, Jimmy. I'm referring to conventions.

J : You mean Moral Conventions?

R : Don't be daft. Jimmy. I'm talking about events like political conventions. You know the ones that have those horrible soggy mushrooms. Don't you just hate soggy mushrooms with rubber chicken dinners, Jimmy?

J : I knew I shouldn't have asked.

R : But if you don't ask, Jimmy, you'll never learn.

J : Before we review any more book titles, are there any spelling mistakes anywhere on this sheet?

R : There's no problem with m'spelling, Jimmy. The problem is with your incorrect assumptions.

J : I'm sure you're right, so maybe you can help me out.

R : No problem, Jimmy, that's what I'm here for.

J : So Book II will be called *K'un* in Chinese and you call it *Turkey Soup for the Miz-Fortunate Sole,* is that right?

R : Right on, Jimmy.

J : And what will that be about?

R : Well Jimmy, *K'un* means *Mother* and *Earth*, so this will be a guide for *Mizzies* on how to deal with *Miz-Prosperity* and wealth.

J : Naturally! Can I at least presume that the reference to '*Turkey Soup*" is a spoof on the *Chicken Soup for the Soul* books?

R : I'm not at all familiar with those books, Jimmy, but turkey soup is much better than chicken soup any day.

J : Fine, but what does it really mean, and why is it good for the *Miz-Fortunate* Sole?

R : Who said it was good for the *Miz-Fortunate* Sole then, Jimmy?

J : Well, I assume that's what the book will explain.

R : There you go making assumptions again, Jimmy. Do you know what assume means?

J : Yeah yeah, I know, it makes an '*Ass*' out of '*U*' and '*Me*'.

R : That's very clever, Jimmy. I'll have to remember that, but no, it means that you're pretending to understand something you know nothing about, just like a P^3. I can see how it makes you look like an ass, Jimmy, but I don't see how it affects me at all.

J : OK, I'll try not to pretend that I understand anything you say.

R : Y'know Jimmy, that's actually an excellent technique employed by many successful *Mizzies* to heighten their state of humiliation.

J : Really?

R : As you appear to be quite familiar with it, Jimmy, I'm really beginning to think that you are a *Mizzy*.

J : Point taken. No more assumptions.

R : Good plan, Jimmy.

J : And I'm not a *Mizzy*!

R : Right, Jimmy. You're still in the closet then.

J : OK, enough of that. We've already discussed Book III, which is a type of management guide for *Mizzies*. The Chinese word appears to be *Chen*, which means what?

R : *Eldest Son* and *Thunder*, Jimmy.

J : What does that have to do with Miz-Management?

R : It's all about business *Miz-Management* and productivity, Jimmy. *Eldest Son* represents business, and *Thunder* represents productivity.

J : Do you really believe all this stuff?

R : What difference does it make if I do or if I don't?

J : OK, never mind. Perhaps we could move on to Book IV, 'Miz-Adventures on the Road Les Travelled,' which seems to be called *K'an* in Chinese. What exactly does *K'an* mean?

R : It means *Second Son* and *Water* and *Moon*, Jimmy.

J : Dare I guess?

R : I wouldn't chance it, Jimmy. You don't have a very good track record, which is why I should do all the thinking. This one is about *Miz-Recreation*, leisure time, and travel. The *Second Son* represents recreation and *Water and Moon* represents travel.

J : Is there any connection to the book called *The Road Less Travelled*?

R : I don't think so, Jimmy. Les never mentioned that he wrote his own book.

J : Who?

R : Les, Jimmy.

J : Less who?

R : Not Les Who, Jimmy, 'Les S. Moore.' He's an old friend.

J : Less-is-more?

R : No, Jimmy, his name is *Lester Seymour Moore*. This book is based on his adventures and travels, more or less.

J : So 'Les' is the actual name of a person?

R : Aye, Jimmy. What have I been saying to you?

J : I'm not really sure.

R : Pay attention, Jimmy.

J : OK. So what about Book V, *The Joey of Miz-Behaving*?

R : It should be obvious, Jimmy, but since you're having so much difficulty with comprehension, it's about *Miz-Relationships* and family. It's a good thing that you don't need to be able to understand anything to be a good writer.

J : Apparently not. Since I don't understand anything, what is a Miz-Behaving Joey and what does it have to do with the Chinese word *Ken*?

R : *Ken* means *Youngest Son*, which represents love, and *Mountain*, which represents relationships.

J : Well that's enlightening. So what's a Joey?

R : Have you never heard of Australia then, Jimmy?

J : Of course I have.

R : Well then, Jimmy, if you knew anything about the land down under, you'd know that a Joey is a baby Kangaroo that still lives in its mother's pouch.

J : I've heard of a Joey, but I just don't get the connection.

R : You really need to get out more, Jimmy.

J : Australia sounds pretty good about now.

R : A bit far to go for a weekend, Jimmy.

J : So can we flush this out a bit more then?

R : No, Jimmy.

J : When would be a good time?

R : Never, Jimmy.

J : What's the problem?

R : The only time I flush anything, Jimmy, is when I visit the wee Laddie's room.

J : Did I say flush?

R : You did, Jimmy? But I don't think that's what you meant.

J : Probably not. What was it that I meant?

R : Fleshed, Jimmy; like putting flesh on a skeleton to give it form.

J : Of course that's what I meant.

R : Good, Jimmy. Let's move on then.

J : Does that mean I have to wait until we get to that book to make any sense of this?

R : Aye, Jimmy.

J : Since I'm not making any more assumptions, I'm curious to hear your explanation for Book VI, *Miz-Understanding and learning the Importance of Change.*

R : Once again, Jimmy, it's dead simple; it's about *Miz-Intelligence* and education.

J : Another *How to Guidebook*, right?

R : Not *How to Guidebooks*, Jimmy. They're all *How **not** to Guidebooks*. The Chinese word is *Sun*, which means *Eldest Daughter* and *Wood* and *Wind*.

J : That's really helpful. Does the importance of change have anything to do with the *I Ching* being called the Book of Change?

R : Not in the least, Jimmy. It's about spare change.

J : Spare change?

R : There y'go repeating me again, Jimmy!

J : Like when someone on the street asks for spare change?

R : That should be obvious, Jimmy.

J : OK, that's another one over my head. Maybe we can leave that one for the moment. Somehow I don't think I'm ready to make the connection between intelligence and spare change.

R : As you wish, Jimmy.

J : In Book VII, *Miz-Fitness for Smarties,* are Smarties a type of Mizzy?

R : Don't you know anything, Jimmy? Smarties are a type of small round candy—you know, where you save the red ones for last.

J : You don't think this will be confused with the numerous *For Dummies,* guidebooks that are in every bookstore?

R : Only a very strange person, like yourself, Jimmy, could possibly confuse Dummies with Smarties.

J : OK then, but do Smarties really need a guidebook on fitness?

R : Have you not seen the ads on television, Jimmy? You know the one where the Red Smarty plays the drums and such? If anyone needs a fitness guidebook, Jimmy, it's the Red Smarty.

J : Of course, how could I have missed that? Back to my earlier question: is the Red 'Smarty' a Mizzy?

R : Don't be daft, Jimmy! How can a piece of candy be a *Mizzy?*

J : How indeed? So what does the Chinese word *Li* mean?

R : It's all about Health and *Miz-Fitness,* Jimmy. The *Second Daughter* represents health and *Fire & Sun* represents fitness.

J : Thankfully, that brings us to Book VIII, The One Habit of Holy Successful Miz-Believers.

R : Aye, that would be Book VIII, Jimmy.

J : Although the title bears some similarities to a book that you referred to earlier about the seven habits, I'll refrain from making any assumptions about possible connections and simply ask about Book VIII.

R : You're learning, Jimmy.

J : Tell me, Red, what is *the One Habit?*

R : Well Jimmy, first, there's more than one type of habit.

J : Of course, that's obvious to you and me, but our readers might have some difficulty understanding how there can be more than one type of *The One Habit.*

R : It's dead easy, Jimmy. Just like one size doesn't really fit all; there are many different habits.

J : OK then, perhaps you could give an example of one of these habits?

R : Nun, Jimmy.

J : None? At first you said there were many habits, and now you say there are none.

R : Nun, Jimmy! N-U-N. Nun.

J : Nun? You mean like a Catholic Nun?

R : Aye, Jimmy. You're not paying attention!

J : So you don't mean a behavioural habit; you mean a type of costume worn by members of religious orders, such as monks and nuns.

R : Finally you're getting the wax out of your ears, Jimmy.

J : So which habit is *The One Habit?*

R : Whichever one is right for you, Jimmy. Each *Mizzy* decides this for himself or herself.

J : And this will all be explained in Book VIII, is that right?

R : Possibly, Jimmy.

J : What does the Chinese word *Tui* mean?

R : *Youngest Daughter* represents the Soul, Jimmy, and *Marsh* represents religion.

J : That would have been my second guess all right.

R : What's your first then, Jimmy?

J : First what?

R : Guess, Jimmy?

J : Oh that would be—you probably could use another coffee, right?

R : Absolutely not, Jimmy. Enough for one day.

J : OK. Have we covered everything about the eight books?

R : Pretty much for now, Jimmy.

J : So what's next?

R : The eight *Miz-Behavioural* characteristics of Book III. See
you on Saturday, same time—Second Cup on Whyte?

Once again Red made a hasty retreat up the escalator, leaving me to my notes. My fantasy of unearthing any thesis material during my sessions with Red was slowly fading into oblivion. As I glanced over the curious names of Red's eight books, visions of Jack Nicholson's brilliant performance in *'One flew Over the Cuckoo's Nest'* danced through my spinning head. It was time to go home.

Chapter V

The Eight Miz-Behavioural Characteristics of Chen

The first Saturday of November was colder than normal, and the only compelling reason for me to keep walking to the Second Cup was the desire for a nice hot cup of coffee. With the prospect of another session with Red Knech looming before me, I really wished that Second Cup was licensed, so I could also have a double scotch. Preparing for a meeting with someone like Red is impossible, but I must admit that my curious side found something quite fascinating about him. Realizing that I was actually growing anxious to hear more on Red's reckonings, it occurred to me that I may be showing early signs of masochism, and I began to worry that I might actually be a closet *Mizzy*.

I spotted Red sitting quietly in the far corner by the window, without a coffee. I headed straight for the order desk to avoid having to say hello first and then come back for our coffees.

THE EIGHT MIZ-BEHAVIOURS OF MIZ

25 - THE ABDICATOR
Wu Wang - Innocence

24 - THE TERGIVERSATOR
Fu - Return

51 - THE INTIMIDATOR
Chen - the Arousing

3 - THE REPUDIATOR
Chun - Difficulty at the Beginning

27 - THE DEMORALIZER
I - the Corners of the Mouth

42 - THE OBSTRUCTER
I - Increase

17 - THE EQUIVOCATOR
Sui - Following

21 - THE PREVARICATOR
Shih Ho - Biting Through

J : Coffee Red?

R : Hello there, Jimmy. Thanks very much.

J : OK, getting back to where we left off on Tuesday, there are eight books, and we're working on Book III, is that right?

R : Aye, Jimmy.

J : And you call it *"Zan and the Mythical Art of Miz-Management,"* but in the I Ching, it's called *"Chen."*

R : We went over all that last Tuesday, Jimmy.

J : OK so… where do we go from here?

R : It's dead easy, Jimmy. I've got it all written down for you.

J : Oh good, another piece of crumpled yellow paper.

R : Brilliant, Jimmy. Practicing criticism, when someone is trying to help you out is a very effective *Mizzy* technique.

J : Sorry, it wasn't intentional. What is this list?

R : Chapter titles for Book III, Jimmy. What did y'think they were?

J : Well I thought they might be a list of movie titles.

R : What could possibly give you a daft idea like that, Jimmy?

J : Well, one of the titles looks similar to *'The Terminator,'* which, by the way is a great movie.

R : *'The Terminator'* is not on the list, Jimmy.

J : No, but there's another similar title called the *'The Intimidator.'*

R : That's not the same as *'The Terminator,'* Jimmy.

J : True, but it sounds a bit similar.

R : But it's not a movie, Jimmy.

J : Well what about *'The Demoralizer?'*

R : I don't think you get it, Jimmy. None of them are movies.

J : OK OK, no more movies. So what are these weird drawings of snakeheads or turtleheads or whatever they are?

R : What weird drawings, Jimmy?

J : The ones next to each chapter heading?

R : They're not *'turtleheads,'* Jimmy? Those are sophisticated cartoons that depict the *Miz-Personality* and *Miz-Behavioural* characteristics that are associated with the title of each chapter.

J : But they all look the same.

R : Are y'blind, Jimmy? They're completely different. Clearly you got a bit short-changed on your powers of observation.

J : OK. If you say so.

R : It's crystal clear, Jimmy.

J : OK, let's see if I can read this… the eight chapter titles are:
'25 - *The Abdicator, Wu Wang, Innocence*'
'24 - *The Tergiversator, Fu, Return*'
'51 - *The Intimidator, Chen, the Arousing*'
'3 - *The Repudiator, Chun, Difficulty at the Beginning*'
'27 - *The Demoralizer, I, the Corners of the Mouth*'
'42 - *The Obstructer, I, Increase*'

'17 - *The Equivocator, Sui, Following*'
'21 - *The Prevaricator, Shih Ho, Biting Through*'
Is that right?

R : Good, Jimmy. At least you can read.

J : So tell me Red, why is the Chinese word "*I*" used for both the *Demoralizer* and the *Obstructer* and what does it mean?

R : Dammed if I know, Jimmy, I don't speak Chinese.

J : C'mon Red, let's get serious. Where did you find these titles?

R : It's called a dictionary, Jimmy. You should try using one.

J : Well I know what the English words mean Red,
but I don't have a Chinese dictionary.

R : You don't need a Chinese dictionary, Jimmy, just a good English one.

J : I have a dictionary.

R : I'll just bet you do, Jimmy. It's probably one of those
wee ones that only have half the words in it.

J : Well what if it is?

R : You know, Jimmy, you can tell a lot about a
man by the size of his dictionary.

J : That's ridiculous.

R : It is, Jimmy, but I had you going there.

J : OK, so how did you come up with these titles, and what do these lines mean?

R : They're hexagrams, Jimmy. As you should recall, we've already covered
the eight fundamentals of the I Ching. Each one of them has eight *Miz-Behavioural* characteristics associated with it, which forms the basis for
the 64 - *I Ching* hexagrams and the abstruse *T-Hex* pyramid puzzle.

J : There you go again; introducing new contrived words that no one has ever heard of.

R : '*Characteristics*' is hardly a new word, Jimmy,

J : Not that word, the other word that sounded like T-Rex or whatever it was.

R : 'Tee-Hex,' Jimmy. You've never heard of it?

J : No, and I don't think I want to.

R : Fine, Jimmy. Now, the chapter headings are the eight
Miz-Behavioural characteristics of *Chen*.

J : What about '*Tee-Hex*' or did you mean T-Rex?

R : You said you didn't want to know, Jimmy, so just forget it.

J : Sure, now that you've really piqued my curiosity.

R : Really, Jimmy? I suppose you're too young to have
ever heard of the Unknown Comic?

J : You suppose right. Why?

R : That would probably mean that you've never seen
the Gong Show on TV either, Jimmy?

J : Also true, but what's that got to do with this discussion?

R : Well Jimmy, the Unknown Comic used to wear a paper bag on his
head and poke fun at Chuck Barris, who hosted the TV show.

J :   So?

R :   He'd say things like, "how do you keep a jackass in suspense?"

J :   Brilliant!

R :   When Chuck Barris responded with, *"I don't know… how?"* the Unknown Comic replied, *"I'll tell you tomorrow."*

J :   Cute. So you're going to tell me tomorrow?

R :   No, Jimmy. Apparently you don't really want to know.

J :   OK then, why tell me about the Unknown Comic?

R :   No reason, Jimmy. I just like him. He's dead funny you know.

J :   Apparently to some people. Maybe we could get back to our topic, if I knew what it was?

R :   Aye, Jimmy. What was your last note?

J :   I think we were discussing the eight *Miz-Be-havioural* characteristics of *Chen*.

R :   Right, Jimmy.

J :   Is each chapter heading based on the I Ching hexagram in some manner?

R :   Not really, Jimmy, but no one will notice.

J :   Don't you think we need to describe the connection between the titles and the Chinese words?

R :   Not really, Jimmy.

J :   Why not?

R :   Because Jimmy, the connection's a bit ambiguous and it's mostly contrived.

J :   Then why go through all this pretence of connecting it to the I Ching.

R :   To give it credibility, Jimmy.

J :   But if it's not really credible, won't the readers figure this out?

R :   Not likely, Jimmy.

J :   I don't get it. Why not?

R :   Because, Jimmy, all the published definitions are also difficult to understand. There are so many books on the I Ching and dozens of different interpretations of each of the hexagrams, that they can mean pretty much whatever you want them to.

J :   That sounds convenient.

R :   Aye, Jimmy. Isn't it just?

J :   So what you're saying is that any connection is purely coincidental.

R :   Mostly, Jimmy, but not as coincidental as I thought they would be. However, as long as it's contrived in comparison with something controversial, it'll be fine.

J :   Really?

R :   Trust me, Jimmy. It certainly worked well for the Da Vinci Code.

J :   But that book was very thoroughly researched, Red.

R :   It had to be, Jimmy. There are a lot of people out there who know their history, and Mr. Brown knew they'd be reading his book.

J :   OK, so we don't have to do research because the I Ching is not well known by our readers, who will likely be few in number anyway?

R : Lucky for us, Jimmy.

J : OK. I'm sorry I asked. Getting back to the book, what are we supposed to do with these Miz-Behavioural characteristics?

R : As you know, Jimmy, in the world of *Brillies*, it's particularly difficult to achieve and sustain an effective *Miz-Environment*. However, when *Mizzies* read this book, they can learn to adopt some of these behavioural characteristics and apply them in the workplace to help influence and change their environment.

J : Before we get into the specifics, are there any general aspects that apply to all of these characteristics?

R : Brilliant question, Jimmy.

J : Is that a good brilliant or a bad brilliant?

R : That's actually a good one, Jimmy.

J : There's a surprise. And they would be?

R : The inverse, Jimmy.

J : The inverse of what?

R : Of leadership behaviours and the like, Jimmy.

J : Do you mean leadership behaviours or habits that are promoted in a best-selling book on Management?

R : Brilliant again, Jimmy.

J : All right then. Since it's unlikely that our *Mizzy* readers will have read any of those books, should we include some examples?

R : Indeed we should, Jimmy. A few behaviour examples would be good.

J : OK. Which ones?

R : It's your thesis, Jimmy.

J : What do mean?

R : It's OK, Jimmy. I saw them when I flipped through your notes.

J : You read my notes?

R : *Our* notes, Jimmy. We're partners, right?

J : If you wanted to see my notes, you should have had the courtesy to ask.

R : Would you have shown them to me then, Jimmy?

J : Probably not.

R : So what would be the point of asking then?

J : That's just plain deceitful.

R : Just like *Duper*, the *Prevaricator*, Jimmy, Chapter 17.

J : As usual, you're way ahead of me.

R : No matter, Jimmy. You've got a great list of leadership behaviours in your note book there. Let's hear them.

J : What's the point if you already know all the answers?

R : I know your answers, Jimmy, but you don't know mine.

J : What are your answers?

R : The inverse, Jimmy.

J : Oh! So if I give you the conventional behaviours, you'll provide the *Mizzy* equivalent behaviours.

R : Along with the name of each one, Jimmy.

J : OK… I'll play along. Here's the first one, *Congenial* and *Compassionate*.

R : That'll be Chapter 3, Jimmy: *Bumper*, the *Repudiator*, who is *Antagonistic* and *Thoughtless*.

J : Sounds a bit too familiar. OK next: *Reasonable* and *Responsible*…

R : Chapter 25, Jimmy: *Dumbper*, the *Abdicator* and he's completely *Unreasonable* and *Irresponsible*.

J : It must be contagious, 'cause that's how I'm feeling.

R : You're learning, Jimmy, and you're doin' just fine.

J : I don't feel fine, but the next one is *Dependable* and *Sincere*.

R : Chapter 24, Jimmy: *Jumper*, the *Tergiversator,* and he's somewhat *Undependable* and *Disingenuous*.

J : Really? The next one is *Respectable* and *Courteous*.

R : That's Chapter 27, Jimmy: *Damper*, the *Demoralizer,* a very *Disreputable* and *Rude* character.

J : Somehow I can relate to that right now. Anyway, the next one is *Affable* and *Considerate*.

R : Good one, Jimmy. Chapter 51: *Thumper*, the *Intimidator,* a really *Hostile* and *Callous* chap.

J : I bet he doesn't have a lot of friends either, like someone who is *Loyal* and *Supportive*.

R : If *Loyal* and *Supportive* is next, Jimmy, it's Chapter 42: *Hamper*, the *Obstructer,* who is *Disloyal* and *Obnoxious*.

J : Big surprise.

R : Just two more, Jimmy.

J : Right, *Reliable* and *Honest*.

R : Chapter 17, Jimmy: *Duper*, the *Prevaricator* and he's *Unreliable* and *Dishonest*

J : That was a bit unimaginative. Last one. *Organized* and *Decisive*.

R : Chapter 21, Jimmy: *Stupor*, the *Equivocator*. *Disorganized* and *Indecisive*.

J : Two equally uncreative answers in a row, but it's a great game. Hey Red, maybe we should drop the book idea and design a game for *Mizzies*?

R : Why would we do that, Jimmy?

J : Well the creators of Trivia Pursuit made a lot of money.

R : This is nothing like Trivia Pursuit, Jimmy.

J : You're right, Red, Trivia pursuit is fun and we wouldn't want *Mizzies* to have any fun would we?

R : No, Jimmy, we wouldn't.

J : OK then, back to misery. If those are the general behaviours, what are some of the specifics?

R : There are many specifics, Jimmy, like the eight '*Ds*' for example.

J : So we have sixteen general behaviours, but only eight specific habits?

R : Not habits, Jimmy—*signs*.

J : Signs of what?

R : Signs of achievement and progress, Jimmy.

J : Like success?

R : Exactly, Jimmy. Each time one of the eight '*Ds*' is evidenced in the workplace; a *Miz-Manager* knows that she has chalked up another goal on the *Miz-Environment* scoreboard.

J : Are these eight '*Ds*' some sort of measure of behavioural success?

R : That's a definite *Red Light,* Jimmy.

J : Red Light?

R : Aye, Jimmy, just like in a hockey game.

J : You mean the red light that goes on when a goal is scored?

R : That's it, Jimmy. Y'see, the measure of *Miz-Success* is not just how a *Miz-Manager* behaves, but how a *Miz-Manager* is perceived. So when there are signs of any of the eight '*Ds*' materializing at work, they act like red light signals to let *Miz-Managers* know that they are making progress towards their long term *Miz-Environment* objectives.

J : Really. So what are these magic eight "*D*" words?

R : Simple, Jimmy. Miz-Success is dependent on a the Miz-Management Team being looked on with various degrees of Disdain, Distrust, Detestation, Denigration, Disrespect, Duplicity, Derision and Deceit.

J : Wow! That could be tough for any *Mizzy,* or even a whole *Miz-Management Team* for that matter, to be perceived from all of the eight "*D*" perspectives.

R : Indeed, Jimmy. But it's not necessary to aspire to all eight. Three or four are usually more than sufficient.

J : Still...

R : Just think how *Miz-Successful* many politicians have become from being perceived by as few as a 3 *D* perspectives.

J : Oh good, we now have another type of 3-D to contend with. I suppose that achieving a 4-D or 5-D perspective would be quite effective.

R : An extreme *8-D* perspective is seldom achieved, except perhaps by a few ruthless Dictators.

J : Isn't that a bit extreme?

R : It is, Jimmy, but you must admit, they have created some very effective *Miz-Environments*.

J : True. And unfortunately many lives have been lost or ruined in the process, and a lot of good people have been badly hurt.

R : We're not endorsing extremism, Jimmy, just pointing out examples.

J : Good. So how does a *Mizzy* determine the most appropriate behaviour to aspire to?

R : Well Jimmy, it doesn't really matter, but regardless of how a *Miz-Manager* strives to be perceived, plans can be thwarted by unpredictable events or by well meaning, misguided *Brillies* and *Sleepers*. In the business world there are even professionals who are constantly developing counter measures to disrupt the progress of *Miz-Management*.

J : Like who?

R : OD consultants and the like, Jimmy.

J : OD consultants?

R :   Organizational Development Professionals, Jimmy. They are always skulking about, trying to steal new ideas for their seemingly inexhaustible supply of fancy charts, behavioural tests, and Power Point Presentations.

J :   Are they the ones who conduct all those touchy-feely workshops?

R :   Aye, Jimmy. The tools of their trade, which they relentlessly employ to lure unsuspecting corporate and government executives into the web of organizational effectiveness and performance improvement.

J :   I take it you've participated in some of these types of workshops?

R :   Dozens, Jimmy, including TQM, JIT, TPM, Sigma Six, The Six Hats, and The Seven Habits, to name but a few.

J :   Although I'm a bit too young to remember when most of them were introduced, in our business classes, we had to learn about Total Quality Management, Just-In-Time, Total Productive Maintenance and all the rest.

R :   Great, Jimmy. So I don't have to try to explain them.

J :   Should we give our readers a bit of an overview?

R :   No, Jimmy.

J :   Why not?

R :   For starters, Jimmy, I don't understand them and can't explain them, and also, they're all on the internet anyway.

J :   OK, but do you know if they are very effective?

R :   You tell me, Jimmy, you're the one who studied them.

J :   But, you said you attended the workshops.

R :   Aye, Jimmy, I did.

J :   Well?

R :   Well what, Jimmy? You can't expect me to remember anything from a workshop that I probably slept through.

J :   I don't suppose that would stop you from having a reckoning on them?

R :   Not at all, Jimmy. Generally, ODs are quite harmless, but in their inexorable quest for clients, they can be quite devious, and it would not surprise me to find some of them actually reading our book when it's finished.

J :   Why would they read it, if they're not *Mizzies*?

R :   To learn the secrets, Jimmy.

J :   If we publish a book, then they won't be secrets.

R :   Exactly, Jimmy.

J :   Are you concerned that they might figure out ways to counter your *Miz-Behavioural* characteristics?

R :   There might be few, Jimmy. However, they'd be offended if we mention it.

J :   And we wouldn't want to offend them, would we?

R :   Definitely not, Jimmy. Especially since some OD types can actually be very helpful without realizing it.

J :   How's that?

R :   Y'see Jimmy, when an OD consultant is brought in to any organization; it automatically sends a wave of anxiety through the rank and file.

J :   You mean like in the old days, when they were known as efficiency experts?

R : Right on, Jimmy. An organization's *Anxiety Factor* can be increased significantly by the mere mention of the arrival of such a threat.

J : Anxiety Factor?

R : Right, Jimmy, it's just one of the many factors that *Mizzies* use to measure their progress, when they are building a *Miz-Environment*.

J : Another measure of success?

R : *Miz-Success*, Jimmy.

J : Of course. So you were saying that an efficiency expert can help contribute to a *Miz-Environment*?

R : Aye, Jimmy, they all used to be very serious looking back then. I have no doubt that the slightest hint of a smile would have been a career-limiting move for most of them.

J : They're different today?

R : Quite different, Jimmy. Today they are the purveyors of smiles, the conveyers of optimism, the assayers of the paradigm shift, and the brayers of new vogue idioms.

J : What does that mean in English?

R : Annoying, Jimmy.

J : That definitely sounds annoying.

R : They're quite effective at it, Jimmy.

J : I thought you said they weren't, although they should be for the amount of money they get?

R : Effective as *Mizzy* allies, Jimmy. On the surface an injection of such positive perspectives might seem to be able to counteract our *Miz-Objectives*, but in reality they are more likely to stimulate *Annoyance* and *Frustration*.

J : Really?

R : Indeed, Jimmy. They are the secret allies of *Miz-Management*.

J : OK, I think I get the picture. So what are our goals and objectives?

R : You mean *Miz-Goals* and *Miz-Objectives*, Jimmy.

J : Whatever.

R : We look to sports, Jimmy. ODs love to use sports analogies in their theories of management behaviours.

J : You mean like teamwork, winning strategies and—

R : Exactly, Jimmy.

J : So what sport do we use?

R : Are you really a Canadian, Jimmy?

J : Does that mean hockey?

R : Brilliant, Jimmy. And what are the goals and objectives in hockey?

J : Well some fans think the goal is to start a fight, but of course the real goal is to score enough goals to win the game.

R : That's the objective, Jimmy, not the goal.

J : Winning is not the goal?

R : Aye, Jimmy.

J : So what are the goals?

R : The main goal is to score goals, Jimmy. That's why they call them goals.

J : Didn't I just say that?

R : Not quite, Jimmy. You said the goal is to win the game, which is really the objective.

J : Of course. How brilliant of me.

R : It's dead simple, Jimmy. Just remember what Foster Hewitt is famous for.

J : Who?

R : You're not that young, Jimmy.

J : Just kidding. "He shoots, he scores!"

R : That was brilliant, Jimmy. So, if your main goal is to score enough goals to meet your objective of winning the game, you need to know how to shoot like Gretzky or Crosby, right?

J : I guess.

R : That means practice, Jimmy. Does it not?

J : Of course, but all hockey players practice shoot- ing a lot and they also practice skating—

R : Now you've got it, Jimmy. They have to practice skating, pass- ing, and shooting to score enough goals to meet their objective.

J : To win the game. I get it.

R : I believe you do, Jimmy.

J : So what do *Mizzies* have to practice?

R : Behaviour exercises, Jimmy. Like *Annoying, Hu- miliating, Belittling* and the like.

J : Where do we explain that?

R : *Annoying* is in Chapter 51, Jimmy. *Humiliating* is in Chap- ter 27, and *Belittling* is covered in Chapter 42.

J : I think I've already OD'd on all three.

R : You don't like ODs, Jimmy?

J : OD'd, Red. It means overdosed.

R : I know that, Jimmy, which is why we're done with be- havioural practices for the moment.

J : You mean you've practiced enough *Annoying, Hu- miliating, and Belittling* for one day?

R : You can never practice too much, Jimmy.

J : OK. So what's the next step?

R : We should probably discuss how this book is go- ing to be organized, Jimmy.

J : Well you've already provided all the chapter head- ings, so what is there to discuss?

R : Well Jimmy, in any well-organized book or report, an outline would normally be provided to help the reader understand what the book is all about. Also, there is often a description of how the book is structured and how the subject matter is going to be covered.

J : OK, I guess we can do that.

R : Absolutely not, Jimmy.

J : But you just said—

R : I said it, Jimmy, so you'd understand that we won't be doing that for this book. It would be counterproductive to our objectives.

J : You're confusing me again, Red.

R : You see how it works, Jimmy.

J : No.

R : Well Jimmy, it's much more *Frustrating* if the reader doesn't know exactly where to find anything in the book.

J : They can just go and look in the index.

R : My point exactly, Jimmy! We won't have an index.

J : No index?

R : No, Jimmy. This is an important point to remember when writing reports and books for *Mizzies*.

J : What if the publisher insists?

R : Well Jimmy, it's unlikely we'll ever find anyone who'll actually publish our book anyway.

J : So why are we doing this?

R : We'll self-publish, Jimmy.

J : Really? How much will that cost?

R : Doesn't matter, Jimmy, you can apply for a grant and get the money. However, if we should find ourselves somehow obligated to include an index in this book, just make sure that the content has nothing to do with the chapter title.

J : So far, with your chapter titles, we seem to going in the right direction.

R : Proper numbering helps too, Jimmy.

J : What do you mean?

R : Look carefully at the chapter numbers, Jimmy.

J : Those are chapter numbers?

R : Aye, Jimmy.

J : But they're not in order?

R : Maybe they don't appear to be in order, Jimmy, but they are correct.

J : How can they be correct if they aren't in order?

R : Those are the correct I Ching numbers.

J : But now we have two Chapter 3s.

R : Aye, Jimmy, but one uses a Roman-numeral and the other uses a Hindu-Arabic number.

J : Won't our readers be confused?

R : Exactly, Jimmy. *Confused, Annoyed, Irritated*, and *Frustrated*.

J : A quadruple threat?

R : Indeed, Jimmy. Y'see, *Brillies* can't abide books that ramble on with confusing passages in a disorganized manner. It makes it difficult to find anything and frustrates them, so they soon lose interest. *Mizzies*, on the other hand, cherish these factors.

J : So only Mizzies will want to read this book?

R : Maybe not, Jimmy.

J : Why would a Brillie want to read it?

R : Well Jimmy, if a friend gifted a *Brillie* the book and told them
     it was really great, they would probably read it, right?

J : But these so-called *'friends'* would have to be deceitful liars, wouldn't they?

R : That they would, Jimmy, but that's what *Pretend Friends* are for.

J : Pretend friends? Why do you call them that?

R : They rhyme, Jimmy.

J : Good; what does it mean?

R : They pretend to be friends, Jimmy, but they don't really like each other.

J : Sounds like a few in-laws I know.

R : Quite right, Jimmy; or *Mizzies*?

J : Perhaps we need the assistance of some OD Consul-
     tants to show us how to organize the book, and then we
     can just ignore their advice or do the exact opposite.

R : Now you're thinking, Jimmy; that really is brilliant.

J : Just kidding, Red.

R : No no, Jimmy, you're finally starting to get it, but of
     course, it will cost you a lot to engage a consultant.

J : Cost me? I don't have any money.

R : Well I can't afford it, Jimmy, so we'll just have to borrow from their books.

J : Now you have me confused again—and just a bit worried.

R : That's exactly the point, Jimmy. *Mizzies* thrive on *Confusion* and *Anxiety*.

J : And we don't want to disappoint them, do we?

R : Of course we do, Jimmy. *Disappointment* can make a major con-
     tribution towards building an effective *Miz-Environment*.

J : So do we need the help of an OD Consultant or not?

R : No, Jimmy, they don't consciously do *Disappointment* very effectively.

J : They do it unconsciously?

R : Unintentionally, Jimmy.

J : Of course. Well I'm feeling disappointed already, so I guess I
     don't have much in common with an OD Consultant.

R : Maybe not, Jimmy, but one thing that *Mizzies* have in common with OD
     Consultants and pretentious scholars is that they all seem to like books
     that begin with an ostentatious and incomprehensible introduction.

J : And you want me to write one for this book?

R : Aye, Jimmy.

J : Unfortunately, I don't have much of an aptitude for that type of
     embellishment, so why don't we just introduce the book with
     your *Annoyance Factor*—in very simple terms of course.

R : Great idea, Jimmy. I just happen to have it written out for you.

J : But Red, this paper's not yellow?

R : Of course not, Jimmy. Does it have a drawing on it?

J : No.

R : Then it's white paper, Jimmy.

J : No drawings… white paper?

R : Right, Jimmy.

J :   Got it. How could I have not known that?

R :   Just read it, Jimmy.

J :   I *am* reading it.

R :   I can't hear you, Jimmy.

J :   You want me to read it out loud?

R :   Aye, Jimmy, out loud.

J :   OK then.

'When assessing the level of organizational disenchantment, the Annoyance Factor serves as a valuable eudemonistic measure. However the key to effective Miz-Management lies in delving to the root of operational harmony and undermining accomplishment, achievement and success by maximizing dysfunctional personal relationships.'

R :   What do y'think, Jimmy?

J :   Do you have an English version?

R :   That would be English, Jimmy, if you'd just learn to pronounce it correctly.

J :   It's my accent, right?

R :   Aye, Jimmy.

J :   And you wrote that?

R :   Don't be daft, Jimmy. I told you I couldn't write. I simply reworded a paragraph from a reputable OD Consultant.

J :   Who wrote it then?

R :   No idea, Jimmy, but I'm sure it's someone who's reputable.

J :   What was the original quote?

R :   'When assessing the level of organizational proficiency, the Harmony Factor serves as a valuable eudemonistic measure. The key to effective management, however, lies in delving to the root of operational discord and circumventing conflict, dissension and failure by minimizing dysfunctional personal relationships.'

J :   Does that mean the *Annoyance Factor* is the opposite of the *Harmony Factor*?

R :   More or less, Jimmy.

J :   So you didn't exactly coin that term *Annoyance Factor,* you simply modified the term *Harmony Factor,* which you borrowed from some anonymous, but famous OD consultant, whose name you've forgotten .

R :   Sounds brilliant, Jimmy, when you put it that way. I don't pretend to be particularly creative either; I'm just an observer of human behaviour, and I like to borrow from the best.

J :   Well, it sounds relatively incomprehensible.

R :   Aye, Jimmy, and the meaning is equally ambiguous.

J :   That should really confound and irritate the reader.

R :   Absolutely, Jimmy. And the added factor is that it brings credibility to the equation which will allow us to conduct a meaningless analysis of the statement.

J :   Which does what, exactly?

R :   *Frustration,* Jimmy, it fosters one of the 24 *Miz-*

Goals: to cause people to be *Frustrated.*

J : No doubt, but we can't just use a quote without permission, especially when it is from someone who we don't even know.

R : You have a problem with that, Jimmy?

J : That would be plagiarism and an infringement of copyright laws.

R : Well Jimmy, you don't have to be an OD consultant to postulate such theoretical drivel, as long as it sounds authoritative.

J : You expect me to write like that?

R : Aye, Jimmy.

J : You seem to be pretty good at it, maybe you should write those parts.

R : It's not my cup of tea, Jimmy, and it's your thesis.

J : Great, but what's the point?

R : Well Jimmy, it helps to introduce infrequently used words with obscure meanings to infuse mild *Humiliation* and send the 'A' type personalities scurrying for their dictionaries.

J : I expect they would all have big dictionaries.

R : No doubt, Jimmy, but if you don't want to get a new one, you can always use Reader's Digest.

J : I let my subscription lapse.

R : No problem, Jimmy, the next time you go to the doctor or the dentist, just borrow a few old Reader's Digest copies from the waiting room and select some vaguely familiar *Word Power* phrases.

J : Chances are they won't be the words I'm looking for.

R : That's perfect, Jimmy. It's not really necessary to use the words correctly. In most cases, *Miz-Use* is preferable in order to exacerbate the *Annoyance* factor.

J : I think it's working; my annoyance is being exacerbated already.

R : Great, Jimmy. You see, words like *eudemonistic* may not be exceptionally rare, but as long as they're not in the Microsoft Word Thesaurus they probably won't be familiar to most readers.

J : Right. Frustration, Annoyance, Irritation and—

R : Good, Jimmy. These factors are some of the foundation stones for building an effective *Miz-Environment.*

J : I imagine that you know many ways to create an effective *Miz-Environment.*

R : Well I do work at the Post Office, Jimmy.

J : What can I say?

R : Some are quite common, Jimmy. For example, simply leaving the toilet seat up or hanging pantyhose to dry over the bathtub can create frustration at home.

J : Talking to you seems to work equally well.

R : Good one, Jimmy, but in this case, you know exactly who's annoying you.

J : Just kidding, Red.

R : That's disappointing, Jimmy. I thought we were making some progress here.

J : You want me to be annoyed?

R : That's the plan, Jimmy.

J : OK, then I wasn't kidding, you really are annoying.

R : Great, Jimmy. But y'see the problem here; being as I'm the perpetrator of the annoyance in this personal relationship, I have no anonymity.

J : It's a bit difficult to have anonymity in a personal relationship.

R : Exactly, Jimmy, and often this can escalate into a premature termination of the relationship.

J : One can only hope.

R : Except, Jimmy, this would end any further opportunities for *Frustration* and *Annoyance*.

J : True Red, but most people have jobs to go to where they can usually experience a fair amount of frustration and the like.

R : Good point, Jimmy. But lack of anonymity can also be problematic in the workplace.

J : In what way?

R : For example, Jimmy, not returning phone calls, not answering e-mails, missing deadlines, being late for meetings. These all generate a considerable amount of *Frustration* and *Annoyance*, but they can't be done anonymously.

J : If you should happen to miss our next meeting, I promise not to be annoyed.

R : That's because you're a closet *Mizzy*, Jimmy.

J : No, I'm not.

R : Aye, Jimmy. You're a classic case. You may convince yourself that something doesn't annoy you, but that's because you're actually relishing in a *Miz-Experience*.

J : That's ridiculous.

R : That's denial, Jimmy. You're only pretending that it doesn't annoy you because you can't tell the difference between feigned patience and *Miz-Enjoyment*.

J : Miz-Enjoyment? I think I've probably had about as many *Miz-Experiences* as I can handle for one day. I wouldn't want to overdo it.

R : Quite right, Jimmy. Even the police have limits on the number of donuts they can have at one sitting. Well I'm off on Tuesday, Jimmy, so I'll see you at the Telus Second Cup. Same time?

With that rapidly delivered terse closing rhetorical question, Red once again quickly rose from his chair, patted me gently on the shoulder and headed for the door like a man on a mission. Although technically he didn't walk out in the middle of a sentence, he did exit while the period was still hot. As the left side of my brain breathed a sigh of relief, the right was feeling mysteriously rejected, wanting desperately to bring some kind of conclusion to this discussion.

For a moment I flashed back to my number one reason for moving out on my own. I had missed the ending of more TV shows because of my brother's uncanny instinct for changing channels at the most crucial point of the show. Suddenly, while my flashback was being replaced by a curious empathy with Chuck Barris, I became conscious of being deserted and realized that it was time to close my notebook and go home.

CHAPTER 25

THE ABDICATOR
(DUMBPER)

WU WANG
INNOCENCE
[The Unexpected]

Abdicate
To give up or renounce one's responsibilities

Tuesday afternoon soon arrived, and I found myself slowly approaching Telus Plaza with an overwhelming compulsion to turn around and run. This self-preservation instinct increased with each step, yet I continued. Unfortunately, logic and reason succumbed to the overpowering lure of the almighty coffee fix, and I sheepishly abandoned my last opportunity to escape.

What if Red was right, and I really was becoming a *Mizzy*? Clearly only a masochist would be willing to spend this much time with Red Knech. On the other hand, desperation has been known to make people do stranger things.

Arriving fifteen minutes early, I was hoping to get there before Red showed up, so I could get myself psyched up for our next encounter. I don't know why I should have been surprised to see Red already sitting at the table by the fake fireplace; after all … thus far, I hadn't successfully predicted anything he had done or said.

J : Red, I didn't expect to see you here already?
R : Then what brings you here so early, Jimmy?
J : Well I thought I'd go through my notes till you got here.
R : Go ahead, Jimmy. I'm not ready anyway.
J : Not ready?
R : For my next coffee, Jimmy.
J : Oh well listen, if you're really not ready, it's OK with me if we postpone this session until next week.
R : No need, Jimmy; I'm good to go now.
J : Are you sure?
R : Absolutely, Jimmy.
J : OK fine. I'll get your coffee.
R : Not now, Jimmy.
J : But I thought you just said you were '*good to go now.*'
R : Aye, Jimmy, but not for coffee.
J : Oh! When do you think you might be ready?
R : That'll be at two-o'clock, Jimmy.
J : OK. Do you mind if I get one for myself?
R : Not at all, Jimmy. And you can put my order in as well.
J : I thought you said you weren't ready.
R : I will be, Jimmy.
J : When?
R : At two-o'clock, Jimmy, when the coffee's ready.

Standing in a long line waiting for coffee has always been a little annoying to me, but in this instance I actually felt a sense of relief. I even found myself wishing that the line would be slower than normal. That wish was granted, but I had another wish, which unfortunately was not—Red was still sitting there when the coffee was finally ready.

J : Coffee's here, Red.
R : Thanks, Jimmy. Right on time.

J : On time?

R : Aye, Jimmy, it's two-o'clock.

J : Oh! Right. So it is. How's it going then, Red?

R : That's my question, Jimmy?

J : It is? OK well… I'm fine, Red.

R : Not you, Jimmy.

J : Oh! Sorry… ah…

R : It's good, Jimmy, that you're feeling well, I mean, but how is our book?

J : Oh! Well, since we haven't even started on the first *Miz-behav-ioural* characteristic, I would have to say it's going a bit slow.

R : Right then, Jimmy, let's get to it.

J : OK. I believe we were discussing factors for determining progress when creating a Miz-Environment, such as frustration, annoyance and the like.

R : Aye, Jimmy, we were.

J : So can you outline some of the techniques for creat-ing frustration in the work environment?

R : Not now, Jimmy.

J : Not now?

R : No, Jimmy.

J : When?

R : When we get to *The Prevaricator*, Jimmy.

J : Which is…?

R : Chapter 21, Jimmy.

J : Chapter 21? Where are we now?

R : Chapter 25, Jimmy: *The Abdicator*.

J : And Chapter 25 comes before Chapter 21?

R : No, Jimmy, it comes before Chapter 24: *The Tergiversator*.

J : OK so… Chapter 25 comes before Chapter 24? What about *Annoyance*?

R : Chapter 51, Jimmy: *The Intimidator*.

J : Do you have a chapter on patience?

R : No, Jimmy, why do you ask?

J : I think I'm losing mine.

R : That's progress, Jimmy, but it's still not a *Miz-Virtue*.

J : Big surprise. So where are we?

R : Chapter 25, Jimmy. This is a very effective *Miz-Behav-ioural* characteristic, and it's called the *Abdicator*.

J : So we are working on Chapter 25, *The Abdicator*?

R : You're repeating yourself again, Jimmy. I gave you a list of the chapters, so please pay attention.

J : Sorry. OK… Why is he called the *Abdicator*?

R : He's not, Jimmy. He's called *Dumbper*.

J : So the Abdicator is called Dumper, right?

R : No, Jimmy.

J : But you just said he was called Dumper.

R : I don't think you pronounced *Dumbper* correctly Jimmy.

J : Dumper, D-U-M-P-E-R, right?

R : As I thought, Jimmy. You missed the 'B'

J : There's no 'B' in Dump.

R : There is in our book, Jimmy. D-U-M-B-P-E-R.

J : Are you kidding?

R : Absolutely not, Jimmy.

J : That's just dumb.

R : That's part of it, Jimmy. But it's not just dumb; it's a combination of dumb and dumper.

J : Cute, Red… like the movie.

R : What movie's that, Jimmy?

J : Never mind, we're not discussing movies anymore.

R : Right, Jimmy.

J : So what is this chapter called then?

R : *Abdicator* is the official name of the chapter, Jimmy.

J : Why is that?

R : Because an *Abdicator* abdicates, Jimmy. Surely you're familiar with the word?

J : Of course, and I'm sure everyone is familiar with this word, but our readers will need to know a little more about how an abdicator can contribute to creating an effective Miz-Environment.

R : Good point, Jimmy. They're BLDs.

J : BLTs? Like in a Bacon Lettuce and Tomato sandwich?

R : It's 'D' Jimmy. B – L – D.

J : What does that stand for?

R : Blamers, Losers and Dumbpers, Jimmy.

J : Blamers, Losers and Dumpers? Sorry. I know, I'm repeating myself again.

R : Indeed you are, Jimmy, but at least you're learning. Now, *Abdicators* are perceived as being a bit dumb, and because they also dump all their work and responsibilities on other people without any explanation, guidance, or assistance, they're called *Dumbpers*.

J : So are they Abdicators or Dumbpers?

R : Both, Jimmy.

J : Why do they need two names?

R : It's like plants and drugs, Jimmy. You know they have their official, Latin name, which no one can remember and then they have their common name.

J : So, I take it that, 'abdicator' is the official 'Latin' name, which I can remember and 'dumbper' is the common name, which isn't a real word.

R : Close enough, Jimmy.

J : OK. So that's dumbping? How do these dumbpers make things happen so they can blame someone else?

R : Brilliant, Jimmy. They misplace important information and blame it on someone else when things go wrong.

J : So dumbping and blaming makes them losers, right?

R : Not at all, Jimmy.

J : They don't sound like winners.

R : Of course not, Jimmy.

J : But you just said they're not losers.

R : Aye, Jimmy, but you meant the ones who aren't winners.

J : There's another type?

R : I just explained it to you, Jimmy.

J : I guess I missed it; what are they?

R : They lose stuff, Jimmy

J : Oh? What kind of stuff?

R : Mostly important stuff, Jimmy.

J : Makes sense. Not much point in losing unimportant stuff, is there?

R : No, Jimmy, there's not.

J : I hope you don't think I'm very important.

R : Why's that then, Jimmy?

J : Well if you consider me to be 'important stuff,' then that would make you a loser…'cause you just lost me *again*.

R : Brilliant, Jimmy. You're doing it then.

J : Doing what?

R : Blaming me, Jimmy, for losing yourself.

J : Of course. How clever of me. So how does one aspire to become proficient at BLDing?

R : What's BLDing, Jimmy?

J : Isn't that what we're talking about?

R : I don't think so, Jimmy. BLDing is not a real word, and it doesn't make any sense.

J : Here we go again. OK. So how does a Miz-manager become a proficient abdicator?

R : To start with, Jimmy, they have to stop always trying to be so reasonable and understanding.

J : So you mean they have to be jerks and assho—

R : Hold on Jimmy! We can't use *those* types of words in this book; the words you're looking for are *Contemptible, Despicable and Disreputable.*

J : Really? So we have to use formal terminology, instead of commonly understood real words?

R : It's a family book, Jimmy. No need to be vulgar.

J : A family book? That's ridiculous. I don't think this will make a good bedtime story, unless we're trying to put someone to sleep.

R : Brilliant, Jimmy.

J : OK… getting back to your behavioural suggestions, that might be easy for someone who is already a complete jerk, but what if our readers don't have a natural aptitude for this type of behaviour?

R : Well Jimmy, y'don't have to be naturally disdainable to be perceived with *Disdain.*

J : Disdainable? Is that a real word?

R : Naturally, Jimmy.

J : Naturally. So is the objective of an abdicator to be perceived with disdain by being contemptible, despicable and disreputable?

R : No, Jimmy. *Dumbper's* intent is to create an *Exploitive Miz-Environment*, and when she sees signs of *Disdain* in the workplace, she knows she's getting there.

J : Definitely not a very common goal for most people.

R : But that's not the goal Jimmy, that's the objective.

J : That's a relief, 'cause it would be a really tough goal.

R : Remember we discussed Goals and Objectives, Jimmy?

J : Oh right, the hockey analogy. So what are *Dumbper's* goals?

R : Practice first, Jimmy.

J : Practice what?

R : What were we just talking about, Jimmy?

J : BLD?

R : That's it exactly, Jimmy. Practice *Blaming*

J : That's *Dumbper's* goal?

R : No, Jimmy, it's one of the behavioural practices that generates actions required to meet goals.

J : So what are these actions?

R : To *Distress* people, Jimmy, so they will meet the goals of feeling *Anguished, Upset, Anxious* and *Distraught.*

J : I don't get it.

R : It's like hockey, Jimmy. Shooting is what you practice so you can take action in a game to shoot. And if you put the puck in the net?

J : You get a goal.

R : Precisely, Jimmy. The red light goes on, and you know for sure. So you practice blaming to distress, and when people are distressed, the red light goes on and you know you've met one of your goals.

J : What red light?

R : *Miz-mms,* Jimmy.

J : What are miz-mms?

R : Signs of Perfidious Negativisms Jimmy.

J : What the hell does that mean?

R : Careful there, Jimmy. Watch the language.

J : Sorry, but I'm lost again.

R : That's the attitude, Jimmy.

J : There's nothing wrong with my attitude.

R : I'm not talking about your attitude, Jimmy. That's the attitude of the *Abdicator.*

J : You mean *Dumbper* has to develop an attitude of Perfidious Negativism?

R : Aye, Jimmy. Do you need to check your wee dictionary there?

J : No. But, what good will an attitude adjustment do?

R : It's necessary, Jimmy, to fuel actions and to counter the attitude of the *Dumbper's* Nemesis.

J :   Which is?

R :   Infectious Enthusiasm, Jimmy.

J :   What do you mean about attitude fuelling actions?

R :   It's obvious, Jimmy. The attitude with which you act has a significant impact on the results.

J :   For example?

R :   Well Jimmy, if a hockey player shoots with apathy, what do you think the results will be?

J :   Pathetic.

R :   Exactly, Jimmy. Y'see it's very difficult to cause much distress with an attitude of honesty and positivism.

J :   I see. But with an attitude of perfidious negativism, one could change the world, right?

R :   Not the world, Jimmy, just the work environment.

J :   You still haven't explained Miz-mms?

R :   Later, Jimmy; I'm not ready to discuss them now.

J :   OK fine. So what are some of the other behavioural practices for *Dumbpers*?

R :   Losing and Dumbbing, Jimmy.

J :   And the actions?

R :   *To Exasperate* Jimmy. This is the action required to make people feel *Irritated, Infuriated, Aggravated* and *Vexed.*

J :   You mean like me?

R :   What's that, Jimmy?

J :   Irritated and lost?

R :   That's the spirit, Jimmy. That's the goal of *Losing.*

J :   What about Dumbbing?

R :   *To Burden,* Jimmy. This is the action required to ensure that *Dumbper's* staff will be *Exhausted, Tired, Fed up, Drained* and *Worn Out,* and that's the last of *Dumbper's* offence goals.

J :   Wow! I better dust off my resume right-a-way so I can apply to work for dumbper.

R :   Sounds idealistically *Mizerable,* doesn't it, Jimmy?

J :   It really does. Eternal Bliss.

R :   *Miz-Bliss,* Jimmy. But unfortunately, it's not eternal.

J :   Are you sure?

R :   Well, as Lincoln once said: You can make all the people *Mizerable* some of the time and some of the people *Mizerable* all the time, but you can't make all the people *Mizerable* forever.

J :   Lincoln never said that.

R :   Maybe not, Jimmy, but he would have, if had been a *Mizzy.*

J :   So… getting back to the now, if those are the offence goals, are there some other goals.

R :   Defence, Jimmy.

J :   Sounds like more hockey talk.

R : Exactly, Jimmy. One defence action is to *Affront*, to meet the goal of causing people to refer to you as being *Contemptible*.

J : Sounds defensive all right. Any others?

R : To *Provoke*, Jimmy, so you can meet your second defence goal of being perceived as *Despicable*.

J : Really! That's one heck of a defence plan. So what are we defending anyway?

R : The *Miz-Environment*, Jimmy.

J : Against?

R : *Brillies*, Jimmy. Who else would it be?

J : Right. Who else? The ones with Infectious Enthusiasm?

R : Quite right, Jimmy.

J : So in addition to practicing behaviours and changing his attitude, what other tricks does dumbper have to learn?

R : Behaviour modification, Jimmy.

J : Didn't we just cover behaviours?

R : Those were behavioural practices, Jimmy, not modifications.

J : What does that mean exactly?

R : That's Unreasonable and Irresponsible, Jimmy.

J : C'mon Red, it was a very reasonable question.

R : It was, Jimmy. As was my answer.

J : What answer?

R : What I just said, Jimmy; *Dumbper* must learn to be *Unreasonable* and *Irresponsible*.

J : Oh! Got it. So, if I was unreasonable and irresponsible, would I be an effective Abdicator?

R : It depends on how *Unreasonable and Irresponsible* you behave, Jimmy.

J : OK. If I was really unreasonable and irresponsible?

R : Well Jimmy, that would certainly go a long way to help you earn *Disdain* in the workplace.

J : You expect me to earn disdain?

R : You're getting there, Jimmy.

J : Is that like the opposite of earning respect?

R : More or less, Jimmy.

J : OK, so in addition to modifying my behaviour to be unreasonable and act irresponsibly, while practicing blaming, losing, and dumbping, now I have to earn disdain to become an Abdicator?

R : Eventually, Jimmy, because developing these behaviours and practices, especially *Dumbping*, contributes significantly to earning the *Disdain* of your staff and colleagues, which in turn creates an *Exploitive Miz-Environment*.

J : Is an Exploitive Miz-Environment another objective?

R : One objective level higher, Jimmy.

J : What's an objective level?

R : In hockey, Jimmy, the first objective is to win the game. The next level objective is to win enough games to take the pennant or at least make the playoffs, while the third level is to win the Stanley Cup.

J : Right. So Dumbper has to practice BLD and earn disdain by acting unreasonable and irresponsible, so he can win the Mizery cup, is that it?

R : It's not quite the same as winning the Stanley Cup or the Grey Cup, Jimmy.

J : Maybe we could call it the Red Cup then?

R : Brilliant, Jimmy. This example of sarcasm clearly demonstrates that you have a real aptitude for mastering the most appropriate use of *Miz-mms* in the workplace.

J : Miz-mms again? What are you talking about?

R : *Miz-mms,* Jimmy. A sign of progress.

J : I give up.

R : Not yet, Jimmy. You're making such wonderful *Miz-Progress?*

J : If that means progressing toward misery, then you're right.

R : Y'see Jimmy, *Dumbper* will know she's achieved her first level objective when there are *Miz-mms* everywhere in the air and her colleagues and staff start referring to her as being *Contemptible* and *Despicable*.

J : Sounds a bit strange to aspire to something like that.

R : Maybe, Jimmy, but that's why *Mizzies* need this book.

J : And why do you keep referring to Dumbper as 'her?'

R : The French word misère is feminine, Jimmy.

J : We're going to get letters, Red, lots of letters, you know that right?

R : From whom, Jimmy?

J : Women, Red. The ones who find that type of comment offensive and sexist.

R : It'll never happen, Jimmy.

J : Why not?

R : No self-respecting woman would be caught dead reading this book, Jimmy.

J : You mean there are no female mizzies?

R : No, Jimmy, but it's unlikely that either of them will ever read this book.

J : Then, back to my original question, why refer to mizzies as her?

R : We won't be sued by any male *Mizzies*, Jimmy, since they're never referred to in our book.

J : What if one or both of the female mizzies actually do read it?

R : Well Jimmy, they would have already reached at least a 4D perspective on us long before they got to this point in the book, so they would most likely have thrown it out in disgust some time ago or given it to a pretend friend.

J : Is disgust the 4th D or would that be the 5th D?

R : Does it matter, Jimmy?

J : I suppose not. But, if no women and no Brillies are going to read this, what's the point of writing it?

R : Some male *Mizzies* are bound to read it, Jimmy, just to relish in the *Miz-Experience*.

J : Well I hope they both enjoy it. In the meantime, what's the first level objective?

R : Suffocation and Repression, Jimmy.

J : Do you mean the objective is to create an environment of suffocation and repression?

R : Not an environment, Jimmy—an *atmosphere*.

J : What's the difference?

R : An atmosphere, Jimmy; is a short term objective and an environment is a longer term objective.

J : OK. So what was our environmental objective again?

R : Exploitive, Jimmy.

J : Right. Does our Brillie Nemesis have any goals and objectives?

R : Absolutely, Jimmy.

J : Is that what we need our defence tactics for?

R : Indeed, Jimmy. Most *Brillies*, on the other hand, would probably have inverse actions and goals that strive to *Achieve* something and be *Successful*.

J : But not the abdicator, right?

R : Correct, Jimmy. Their first level objectives are to create an atmosphere of *Liberation* and *Manumission*.

J : Manu-what?

R : *Manumission,* Jimmy, the formal act of freeing slaves. Don't bother with your wee dictionary; it's probably not in there.

J : And what's the Environmental objective for Dumbper's nemesis?

R : Expressive, Jimmy.

J : Great. I've changed my mind. I'm sending them my resume. They're probably reasonable and responsible as well.

R : No doubt, Jimmy.

J : Which, by the look on your face, is clearly unacceptable, right?

R : Right, Jimmy. If *Miz-Managers* would only just relinquish their responsibilities and obligations, so they're not accountable for anything and act *Unreasonable* and *Irresponsible* to create an atmosphere of *Suffocation* and *Repression* where *Mizzies* can thrive in an *Exploitive Miz-Environment,* they could achieve amazing *Miz-Results*.

J : Wow. Sounds like heaven.

R : Doesn't it just, Jimmy.

J : The mere thought of basking in an Exploitive Miz-Environment and being showered with the fruits of disdain gives me goose bumps.

R : The *Abdicator* can be amazingly effective at ensuring that those around her maintain a high standard of *Mizery*.

J : It certainly sounds effective. I can easily see how the *Blamies and Dumbpies* might be miserable, but—

R : What are Blamies and Dumbpies, Jimmy?

J : The ones who take the blame or who are being dumbped on.

R : There are no such words, Jimmy.

J : Well, you make up words all the time.

R : Only when there is no word in the dictionary, Jimmy.

J : OK then, I can see how the ones being dumbped on or blamed would be miserable, but how does that contribute to the abdicator's miz-experience?

R : You've heard that misery loves company, Jimmy.

J : Of course.

R : Well, it works both ways, Jimmy.

J : You mean it's contagious?

R : No, Jimmy, it's infectious. *Mizziness* is contagious.

J : Mizziness? Is that anything like dizziness?

R : Dizziness is not contagious, Jimmy.

J : Good, we now know what it's not, but what *is* it?

R : It's when someone feels *Mizzy* or *Mizerable,* Jimmy.

J : How is that contagious?

R : Just like when someone makes you feel sick, Jimmy, or something makes you feel dizzy; someone or something can also make you feel *Mizzy.*

J : So we have one Mizzy making another Mizzy feel Mizzy, is that it?

R : That's the problem, Jimmy. It's not always a *Mizzy* who makes a *Mizzy* feel *Mizzy.*

J : Really?

R : Sometimes it's a *Brillie,* Jimmy. But even though they have a special aptitude for transferring *Mizziness* to others, they are not necessarily *Mizzies* themselves.

J : So what are they?

R : Carriers, Jimmy. They seem to be immune to *Mizziness* and will probably never be *Mizzies* themselves, but they are carriers.

J : Kind of like those folks who will never have a heart attack, but are carriers.

R : Exactly, Jimmy.

J : Right. So all the abdicator has to do is blame others for all their problems, lose important stuff, and dumbp all their work on other people to make everyone feel mizzy?

R : That's it exactly, Jimmy. A lot of *Mizzies* try to adopt this behavioural technique because they've observed how effective it can be for P^3s, who aren't even trying to infect people with *Mizziness* and create a *Miz-Environment.*

J : Sounds simple enough.

R : On the surface, Jimmy, it seems dead easy, especially if you're a *Miz-Manager* who is responsible for managing *Workload* and has the authority to implement it. But it's actually very difficult for most *Mizzies.*

J : Why's that?

R : Well y'see Jimmy, a lot of *Mizzies* put considerable effort into what they do because working hard, while working ineffectively is a time honoured proven technique for ensuring a constant state of *Mizery.*

J : Are you suggesting that hard work is characteristic of some Mizzies, but uncharacteristic of an effective abdicator?

R : Good for you, Jimmy. There's hope for you yet.

J : Lucky guess.

R : The problem is, Jimmy, many *Mizzies* have a hard time do-
    ing nothing, especially because they are workaholics.
J : So some workaholics are *Mizzies*?
R : No, Jimmy.
J : No?
R : All, Jimmy—*all* workaholics are *Mizzies*.
J : But some workaholics seem quite happy.
R : Absolutely, Jimmy. Content with their *Mizery*. For *Mini-Mizzies*, the—
J : *Mini-Mizzies?* Is that a real word?
R : Aye, it is Jimmy.
J : I don't believe it. How come you get to make up new words, but I can't.
R : '*Mini,*' Jimmy, is a legitimate word. It's even in those wee dic-
    tionaries like the one you have. I didn't make it up.
J : OK. I'll bite; what's a Mini-Mizzy?
R : Y'see Jimmy, not all *Mizzies* require the same lev-
    el of *Mizery* to satisfy their needs.
J : You mean each *Mizzy* requires a different dosage of misery?
R : You could say that, Jimmy. Just like food, some need more
    than others to sustain themselves. The '*dosage,*' to use your
    phrase, can range from the mild to the extreme.
J : So would a Mini-Mizzy only need a low dosage?
R : Brilliant again, Jimmy. For some *Mini-Mizzies,* the level of overexer-
    tion caused by workaholic tendencies is often sufficient in itself to
    induce a highly effective *Miz-State*. This usually creates enough *Mizery*
    to satisfy their cravings, which makes them appear to be *Miz-Content*.
J : OK. Now we have 'Mini-Mizzies' and although they're re-
    ally miserable, they appear to be content?
R : Exactly, Jimmy, but we know that they are actually *Mizzies* because
    they constantly complain a lot about everyone and everything.
J : So now we have happy whiners, is that it?
R : Not at all, Jimmy, we have energized whin-
    ers who love to wallow in their own *Mizery*.
J : I think I've exceeded my Miz-Dosage. I need a break!
R : The wee lads room, Jimmy, is the other way.
J : Oh? Thanks.
R : Feeling better, Jimmy?
J : Much. Thanks. OK let's see… I had a question here…
    If they're workaholics, aren't they completely respon-
    sible for creating their own work environment?
R : Y'seem to forget, Jimmy, *Abdicators* have renounced their duties and
    responsibilities so they can't be held accountable for anything.
J : So why do they complain about it?
R : Because, Jimmy, if they don't complain, then everyone will know that
    they're enjoying their *Mizery* and that they probably are *Mizzies*.
J : That's scary.

R : No, Jimmy? *Mini-Mizzies* aren't at all scary.

J : No, I don't mean that Mizzies are scary. What's scary is that I'm having difficulty challenging your logic, which either means I'm tired or this stuff isn't sounding quite as ludicrous as it should.

R : That's called progress, Jimmy.

J : That's even more scary. So now we have determined that some Miz-Managers have difficulty doing nothing.

R : Right, Jimmy, especially *Maxi-Mizzies*.

J : 'Maxi-Mizzies'? I thought we were talking about 'Mini-Mizzies'?

R : Aye, Jimmy, we were, but you brought up the issue of scary *Mizzies,* and *Mini-Mizzies* aren't nearly as scary as *Maxi-Mizzies*.

J : We definitely need a *'Red Knech'* dictionary.

R : It's a Glossary, Jimmy, and you'll be sure to *maxi-size* it then.

J : OK, you don't like my mini dictionary, but what the heck is a 'Maxi-Mizzy'?

R : Check your notes, Jimmy. You wrote it down. 'Mild *Mizzies* and Extreme *Mizzies.*'

J : So?

R : It should be dead obvious, Jimmy. *'Maxi'* means extreme or mega, right?

J : Brilliant.

R : Exactly, Jimmy. *'Mega'* also means brilliant, as well as enormous. You've been reading your wee dictionary.

J : Clearly, I don't have much of a life.

R : Not to worry, Jimmy, our book will keep you busy.

J : OK. Moving on. How can our readers learn to become an Abdicator and learn the techniques of Blaming, Losing, and Dumbping?

R : Good question, Jimmy. For *Miz-Managers* who are already effectively doing nothing, it's relatively easy to achieve *Miz-Success* as an *Abdicator*. In fact, many have already taken the first steps, but most need to sharpen their skills in this area.

J : And for those who have a compelling urge to actually do something?

R : Well Jimmy, the first thing that they have to learn is to appreciate that the very act of restraining themselves can generate a whole new *Miz-Experience*.

J : How's that?

R : Restraint, Jimmy, can be extremely stressful for most *Miz-Managers,* and high levels of stress can enhance their *Miz-Experience* to amazing heights.

J : What exactly should they restrain themselves from doing?

R : Their jobs, Jimmy.

J : You mean like what's outlined in their job descriptions?

R : Precisely, Jimmy, if they have a job description. And they must stop interfering.

J : Interfering in what?

R : In the work that their staff is supposed to do, Jimmy.

J : Does that include the work that they dumbp on their staff?

R : Especially the dumbped work, Jimmy. Even though it's extremely important to *Miz-Managers* to ensure that everything gets messed up regularly and properly, they must learn to resist their instinct to interfere with the work they've dumbped on others.

J : Why would they feel that they have to interfere anyway?

R : Questions, Jimmy.

J : That was a question.

R : No, Jimmy. It's the asking of the questions.

J : It shouldn't be very difficult to resist asking questions about work they've dumbped on their staff.

R : It's not them asking, Jimmy; it's them answering. They must learn to resist answering any questions about the work they *Dumbp*.

J : What if the employee is insistent?

R : That's easy, Jimmy, just remind them that it's their area of expertise or that it's their responsibility.

J : Even if it's not their responsibility.

R : Especially if it's not, Jimmy.

J : What if they just can't resist interfering?

R : That's just it, Jimmy. *Miz-Managers* are naturally attracted to activities that they don't like or that they aren't good at. They just need to be made aware of the *Miz-Benefits* of self-restraint.

J : Should I bother asking what Miz-Benefits means?

R : Isn't it obvious, Jimmy?

J : We'll add it to the list of words for the glossary. So… what if some people find it very hard to resist the temptation to interfere?

R : Then that's perfect, Jimmy, because when workaholic *Miz-Managers* really get to experience how wonderfully *Mizerable* it feels to resist the temptation to interfere with the work of their employees, they soon learn to become very effective *Dumbpers*.

J : What if it doesn't work?

R : Well Jimmy, if this is new for their staff and, in a worst-case scenario they have been cursed with effective and loyal employees, it may take a wee bit of time before their employees start to become *Upset, Exasperated and Exhausted*.

J : Do you mean that some employees might step up to the plate and actually do the work that gets dumbped on them?

R : The *Mizzy* staff usually do anyway, Jimmy, but they aren't the real problem.

J : Why's that?

R : Because, Jimmy, they'll do it the way it needs to be done.

J : What way is that?

R : Wrong, Jimmy.

J : I suppose it's the *Brillies* who are the problem then?

R : Exactly, Jimmy, and if they are really loyal and competent employees, then it's quite possible that they might actually do what they are told to.

J : Could be disastrous.

R : But not to worry, Jimmy, it doesn't usually last very
long before they get fed up and exasperated.

J : What if it *does* take quite a while?

R : *Impatience,* Jimmy, is a *Miz-Virtue* since it can contribute significantly to one's *Miz-Environment* when one is forced to be patient.

J : I suppose you expect me to ask about other *Miz-Virtues*?

R : That's the whole point of this book, Jimmy. But we'll have to
take it one subject at a time so you don't get lost again.

J : And if impatience doesn't work?

R : Blame, Jimmy. Adding blame to the equation can accelerate the process.

J : How can you blame your staff if they're doing a good job?

R : Who's the boss, Jimmy?

J : The Manager?

R : The *Miz-Manager,* Jimmy. And doesn't the boss determine if the employee is doing a good job or not?

J : I suppose. So if they've done a good job, the *Miz-*
Manager simply tells them it's not good?

R : Not at all, Jimmy. The *Miz-Manager* simply tells them to do it
again and provides them with appropriate *Miz-Direction.*

J : Miz-Direction? Good, another new word for the glossary. So if they
get brilliant *Miz-Direction*, then it will get redone incorrectly?

R : Bingo, Jimmy. If someone senior or outside the department grumbles
about it being wrong, the *Miz-Manager* simply blames the employee
and then provides the original correct version along with a complaining comment such as, *'I always have to do everything myself.'*

J : Like I've never heard *that* one before. However, some
people might think that's unethical and unfair.

R : We'll get to that in Chapter 21, Jimmy.

J : Get to what?

R : Ethics, Jimmy. But what's that got to do with anything, and whoever said life was fair anyway?

J : Apparently it wasn't a *Mizzy.*

R : Clearly not, Jimmy. But remember, the objective here is to foster an effectively dysfunctional workplace environment, called a *Miz-Environment*
where everyone can relish in the experience of communal dissonance.

J : Of course, how could I have missed that one? Well, I suppose if everyone in the department was a *Mizzy* that might
be OK until the company goes out of business.

R : That's the problem, Jimmy.

J : Going out of business?

R : That too, Jimmy. But the real problem is that not everyone is a *Mizzy.*

J : That's a real problem all right.

R : Not if you know how to solve it, Jimmy, which is the point of this book.

J : So you have the solution?

R : Absolutely, Jimmy.

J :   I can hardly wait?

R :   Patience, Jimmy.

J :   Patience is the solution?

R :   Don't be daft, Jimmy. It's you that needs the patience.

J :   I agree. I could definitely use more patience, but it's not a *Miz-Virtue*.

R :   It's not that difficult, Jimmy. All that *Dumbper* has to do is ensure that the *Brillies* are constantly *Upset, Exasperated,* and *Exhausted*. Their negative reaction to this condition is guaranteed to contribute to, and enhance, the quality of the *Miz-Environment*.

J :   You mean like 'misery loves company?'

R :   Not exactly, Jimmy; it's more like *'Misery generates more misery.'*

J :   So dumbing and blaming can be an equally effective technique on both *Mizzies* and *Brillies*?

R :   That's ridiculous, Jimmy. *Dumbping* and *Blaming* have absolutely no effect on *Mizzies,* and *Mizzies* aren't the problem.

J :   Of course, I forgot.

R :   Great, Jimmy, now you're starting to talk like a real *Mizzy*.

J :   Not intentionally.

R :   Maybe not, Jimmy, but statements like *'I forgot'* are trademark phrases in the world of *Mizzies*. The important thing to remember is to be sure that someone else takes the blame.

J :   But if someone says *'I forgot,'* then doesn't it mean that… that person forgot, not someone else?

R :   Not at all, Jimmy. They just need to finish the statement with 'because so-and-so didn't put it in my calendar' or 'so-and-so didn't remind me.'

J :   Oh I see; always blame someone else.

R :   Brilliant, Jimmy. I think you've got it.

J :   Maybe I'll try practicing *'losing stuff'* and see if I can lose it?

R :   Brilliant again, Jimmy. Unfortunately, losing or misplacing things is much more difficult than it used to be before E-Mail.

J :   E-Mail is definitely a pain in the you-know-where.

R :   Not at all, Jimmy. E-Mail can be a major contributor to the enhancement of the *Exasperation Factor*, but *Miz-Managers* need to learn how to take advantage of it.

J :   I certainly see the exasperating side of E-Mail, but what did you mean by losing things was easier before E-mail.

R :   It's a bit obvious, Jimmy. Before E-Mail, it was dead easy to say *'I never got the memo'* or *'it got lost in the mail.'*

J :   Even if it didn't?

R :   Remarkable, Jimmy, you got it again. We used to be able to put stuff in the *'round file'* or slip it into the bottom of someone else's in-box, but with E-Mail, it's more difficult to deny receiving *'the memo'* or whatever.

J :   That is a real dilemma all right, so what can a Dumbper do about it?

R :   Forward it, Jimmy.

J :   Forward to who?

R :   Anyone of her staff, Jimmy.

J :   I should have guessed that one. Are there other things she can do?

R :   Definitely, Jimmy. For example, she can reply with a lot of stupid questions, or make up reasons to be critical of the sender and the content. Another thing is to reply with a bunch of irrelevant attachments or links to large unrelated websites.

J :   Anything but answer the E-Mail with the right information, is that it?

R :   Amazing, Jimmy. You're tuned right into this one aren't you?

J :   It's a pet peeve of mine. So what is the point of learning to be an effective Abdicator?

R :   To build a better *Miz-Environment,* Jimmy. These techniques and characteristics are for the benefit of *Miz-Managers*, to help them counter the actions and attitudes of enthusiastic *Brillies*.

J :   You have a real thing about *Brillies* being the problem, don't you?

R :   Definitely, Jimmy. They are constantly undermining the efforts of *Miz-Managers* who are simply trying to build an effective *Miz-Environment*.

J :   Are the Abdicator's techniques of blaming, losing, and dumbping best suited for Mini-Mizzies or Maxi-Mizzies?

R :   Both, Jimmy, especially workaholic *Mizzies*.

J :   I thought all *Mizzies* were workaholics. Are you saying there are some who aren't?

R :   No, no, Jimmy, all workaholics are *Mizzies*, but not all *Mizzies* are workaholics.

J :   Sorry, I can't believe I got that mixed up.

R :   Y'see Jimmy, there are different degrees. As I said earlier, most low functioning workaholic *Mizzies* have probably already mastered the art of doing nothing rather effectively. They have likely experienced the *Miz-Benefits* of this characteristic trait, but many others just don't use their talents effectively.

J :   That's a shame. Why do you think that is?

R :   Well Jimmy, some are very proficient *Dumbpers,* and others are accomplished *Blamers*. Most are reasonably good at *Losing* stuff, but very few seem to able to master all these skill sets equally well.

J :   Even if *Dumbpers* master these skills, how can they prevent enthusiastic *Brillies* from undermining her efforts?

R :   Spot on question, Jimmy. That's the whole point of our book. As you are aware, there are no self-help books out there for *Mizzies*.

J :   Really? You mean to say there isn't some book called *'Creating Effective Miz-Environments for Miz-Dummies'* sitting on the shelves of every bookstore? How could they have missed that one?

R :   How indeed, Jimmy? Now I think you're beginning to appreciate the real need for our book.

J :   Clearly a void in the market. So what do *Brillies* do to undermine the successful development of a *Miz-Environment,* and how does a *Miz-Manager* counter the effects of *Brillies*?

R :   Brilliant, Jimmy. That is the most brilliant question you've ever asked me.

J :   Was it a good brilliant question or a stupid brilliant question?

R :   Good, Jimmy.

J :   OK then, thanks, I guess.

R :   *Infectious enthusiasm,* Jimmy.

J :   Excuse me?

R :   The answer to your brilliant question, Jimmy.

J :   The answer is 'infectious enthusiasm?'

R :   Precisely, Jimmy. It is possibly the most dangerous character trait of all.

J :   It's a character trait then?

R :   What else would it be, Jimmy? *Infectious enthusiasm* is the *Abdicator's* nemesis.

J :   That sounds like a pretty daunting Nemesis all right.

R :   The worst, Jimmy. A *Dumbper* works hard to develop an *Exploitive Miz-Environment* where repression can thrive, then along comes some *Brillie,* filled with *infectious enthusiasm,* and before you know it, free expression and eagerness start creeping back into the working environment.

J :   And we don't want that, do we?

R :   Absolutely not, Jimmy. It undermines our *Miz-Objective.*

J :   So what are some of the telltale signs of infectious enthusiasm that Dumbper should be watching out for?

R :   Another brilliant question, Jimmy. For example, these insidious characters regularly go the extra mile to resolve difficult problems. They often work out ways and means to improve processes and increase efficiency—,

J :   Hold it, you're going too fast.

R :   And, Jimmy, they commit all kinds of other dastardly deeds, which can lead to the destabilization of the *Miz-Environment.*

J :   Boy, they sound like pretty dangerous characters all right. Are these deceitful Brillies with 'infectious enthusiasm' the only ones to worry about?

R :   If only, Jimmy! But with so many different types of *Brillies,* unfortunately, there is an overabundance of treacherous characteristics to watch out for.

J :   And they would be?

R :   Later, Jimmy.

J :   Later?

R :   We have to save some for the other chapters, Jimmy.

J :   If there is an overabundance of character traits, don't you think we should have more than one per chapter, even if this is the most dangerous?

R :   Good point, Jimmy. They should also watch out for *Brillies,* who really like their work, who seldom complain, rarely take sick time, come in early, stay late, and *worst of all* buy coffee for their colleagues.

J :   Wow! Definitely some pretty bad traits to watch out for. So if Dumbper becomes really good at blaming, losing and, dumbping—

R :   It's called *Hooking,* Jimmy.

J :   Excuse me, did you say Hooking?

R :   Aye, Jimmy, the techniques of *Blaming, Losing* and *Dumb-*

ping are quietly referred to by *Mizzies* as *Hooking.*

J :   Are you sure about using that term?

R :   Dead sure, Jimmy, why?

J :   Because that term is already in common use, and it has other meanings, which are not particularly respectable.

R :   Really, Jimmy?

J :   Yes, really! I can think of two other meanings for that word and one means a jail sentence, while the other means time in the penalty box.

R :   That's it, Jimmy, but the beauty is that there are really no hooking penalties in the workplace because the *Miz-Manager* is the referee.

J :   Are we talking about a *hooking penalty*, like in hockey?

R :   Exactly, Jimmy.

J :   You really are a hockey fan, aren't you?

R :   Fastest game in the world, Jimmy.

J :   I thought all you Brits were into soccer?

R :   It's Football, Jimmy. And not that sissy game you play over here.

J :   OK, fine. But, why is it called hooking?

R :   In hockey, Jimmy, what's a hooking penalty called for?

J :   That's easy; it's for hooking a stick around an opponent to block his progress.

R :   Absolutely right, Jimmy. And *Blaming, Losing,* and *Dumbping* are simply techniques for impeding and blocking the progress of their *Brillie* opponents.

J :   Sounds like a secret code?

R :   That's exactly what it is, Jimmy. Where *Mizzies* are concerned, everything's a secret.

J :   Well what's not a secret is that I think I've just about run out of steam for today and it's getting late.

R :   Almost done, Jimmy. Just the skit to finish.

J :   Skit? What skit?

R :   A skit to exemplify how to use *Hooking* effectively.

J :   Really?

R :   It's very short, Jimmy, and the sooner we start, the sooner we finish. Here, I've written it all out for you.

J :   Oh good, another piece of crumpled paper,

R :   It's quite legible, Jimmy.

J :   OK. Let's go.

R :   So read out the characters then, Jimmy.

J :   Where did you get this stuff?

R :   What stuff, Jimmy?

J :   The ideas and information for this story.

R :   Fairy Tales and Children's stories, Jimmy.

J :   I didn't know that Fairy Tales demonstrated exemplary behaviour for managers?

R :   They don't, Jimmy, but they work for *Miz-*

Managers with a bit of re-writing.

J : So this is a modified Fairy Tale?

R : Right Jimmy. So let's get started.

J : What Fairy Tale is this based on?

R : Cinderella, Jimmy. Can we start now?

J : OK. Lady Renounce is Dumbper; the Admin Assistants are Azmella and Nazeldrip, Cinderella is the clerk, and Lord King is the President.

R : Good, Jimmy. Now read the set up for the skit.

J : Is there a Fairy God Mother and a Prince Charming?

R : No, Jimmy. This is a real life version.

J : Are Azmella and Nazeldrip Lady Renounce's daughters?

R : Do you seriously think, Jimmy, that a reputable real estate office would support nepotism?

J : So Lord King runs a reputable real estate office?

R : No, Jimmy.

J : I thought you just said it was a real estate office.

R : Did I say it was reputable, Jimmy?

J : No but—

R : Right. Now let's get on with it, Jimmy.

J : OK. Once upon a time there was a company in the Magic Kingdom called the Magic Kingdom Real Estate and Property Development Corp. Lord King has asked Lady Renounce to prepare an IAR—What's an IAR?

R : An Investment Analysis Report, Jimmy.

J : Could be confused with the IRA.

R : We're not in Ireland, Jimmy. Now, where were we?

J : Right. Lord King has asked Lady Renounce to prepare an IAR on a downtown property occupied by a 22 year old, 14 storey office building, with 2 levels of underground parking.

R : And Lord King has provided Lady Renounce with what, Jimmy?

J : Let's see here:
A building condition report;
A market analysis of the property;
A building code assessment;
A legal survey, land title registration and zoning regulations;
A financial performance summary of income and expenses for the past five years; A listing of all leases and expiry dates and;
A full disclosure of operating costs, including annual staff, utilities, taxes, operating, and maintenance costs.

R : So that's seven files then, Jimmy.

J : I guess so.

R : So read the next bit then, Jimmy.

J : It's 3:30 on a Wednesday afternoon, and the report is due in Lord King's office on Friday morning. Lady Renounce has had more than two weeks to work on this and has done nothing. Cinderella is a clerk who was transferred from the development office and now reports to Lady Renounce. She has never worked on an investment analysis. She is called into Lady Renounce's office.

R : Now we read the dialogue like a play, Jimmy. I'll be Lady Renounce (LR) and you can be Cinderella (C).

J : Is this really necessary?

R : No, Jimmy. Just humour me.

J : OK.

R : (As LR); Cinderella, get in here. I have a job for you.

J : (As C): What do—

R : Wait, Jimmy, you missed the note.

J : Oh, right. I didn't see it there in the margin. Lady Renounce throws 3 of the 7 files at Cinderella, including the building code assessment; the legal survey, land title registration and zoning regulations and the listing of all leases and expiry dates.

R : Good, Jimmy.

J : So where are the other files?

R : Lost, Jimmy. We'll get to that later. Just read your next line.

J : OK. (As C): What do you want me to do with this?

R : (As LR): I need you to a complete an investment analysis on this property and have it finished by first thing tomorrow morning to be delivered to Lord King.

J : (As C): But it's already 3:30 and I've never done an Investment Analysis before.

R : (As LR): Well then, it's time to learn. You have to earn your keep if you want to eat.

J : (As C): I don't even know where to start. Do you have a copy of a previous report that I could use as a guide?

R : (As LR): Here's a previous IAR you can use. Just do the best you can, but it better be good. Azmella and Nazeldrip, come now we have to go for dinner. Be here first thing in the morning Cinderella, and that report had better be finished.

J : Is this called dumbping?

R : Absolutely, Jimmy. Now we go to the next morning and I'm still Lady Renounce. (As LR): All done Cinderella?

J : (As C): Well I worked all night, and I did the best I could, but I don't seem to have all the information I needed in the 3 files you gave me.

R : (As LR): I distinctly remember giving you seven files.

J : (As C): Well there were just 3 files in the pile.

R : (As LR): You must have misplaced them. Azmella may still have another copy of the other files. She's always moving my files around and re-sorting them. Get Nazeldrip to help you find them for you, and then bring me the finished report by 3:00 o'clock this afternoon

J : Sounds like blaming this time.

R : It does, doesn't it, Jimmy? Now keep reading so we can finish this.

J : (As C): I thought it had to be submitted this morning?

R : (As LR): Is it ready?

J : (As C): No. I—

R : (As LR): Then how can it be delivered this morning if it's not finished. Now I have to beg for an extension. Finish it by 3:00. No excuses this time.

J : (As C): OK.

R : (As LR): and don't forget to e-mail a copy of the pre-liminary report to Lord King for his review.

J : (As C): Should I copy you?

R : (As LR): Don't bother, just leave a copy on my desk.

J : (As C): Cinderella talks—

R : No, Jimmy. That's a note your reading. It says Cinderella talks to Azmella and Nazeldrip about the other files.

J : Oh. So will you be *Azmella* or *Nazeldrip*?

R : No, Jimmy. I only play Lady Renounce, so you'll have to do all the other parts.

J : Do I have to do different funny high voices for *Azmella* and *Nazeldrip*?

R : You're being silly, Jimmy. There's no audience here, just the two of us.

J : (As C): Azmella, do you have the rest of the files for this project?

J : (As A): No, Mommy always keeps them all on her desk.

J : (As C): She said you probably put them down on your desk somewhere.

J : (As A): Mommy is always dumbping stuff on my desk and accusing me of losing them.

J : (As C): Can you help me—

J : (As A): Can't you see I'm busy.

J : (As C): Nazeldrip can you—

J : (As N): Go and look yourself.

R : Now there's another note, Jimmy. Cinderella checks Lady Renounce's desk and finds the files at the bottom of her in-basket. Cinderella heads back to her seat on the floor by the fireplace to finish the report.

J : Sounds like someone's been misplacing files.

R : Not misplacing, Jimmy—*losing*.

J : Right, *losing* important stuff?

R : That's it, Jimmy. Now read the rest of the note.

J : OK. At 2:35, Cinderella provides Lady Re-nounce with a copy of the final draft.

R : (As LR): You took your time.

J : (As C): Well, I think I got what you need, but—

R : (As LR): Whatever. Just send me an e-mail copy, so I can read it on my computer later. I'm busy. Now get out.

J : (As C): OK.

R : There's another note there, Jimmy.

J : Right. Nazeldrip comes into Lady Renounce's office and ad-vises Lady Renounce that Lord King is here looking for her. Lady Renounce runs down to greet Lord King.

R : Good, Jimmy. Now you can be Lord King.

(As LR): Greetings Your Majesty.

J : (As Lord King): Lady Renounce, what's this IAR that I got from this Cinderella person? Have you actually read it? Its garbage, Lady Renounce. What's going on down there anyway?

R : (As LR): Sorry your majesty, I don't know what you're referring to.

J : (As Lord King): Didn't you have this report sent to me?

R : (As LR): I don't recall even seeing a copy your majesty.

J : (As Lord King): Oh, right. I see here that you weren't even copied on this e-mail Lady Renounce. So what's happening with the report, and who is this Cinderella?

R : (As LR): I'm just finishing the report myself your majesty, and I'll personally deliver it to your palace by midnight.

J : (As Lord King): You must know how important it is to have this report for the board meeting tomorrow.

R : (As LR): Of course your majesty. I won't let you down.

J : (As Lord King): I'm depending on you Lady Renounce. So who is this Cinderella anyway?

R : (As LR): She's just one of my lowly clerks, your majesty , transferred from the Development Group. She was helping out with the research on this project. She wants a chance to show off her talents.

J : (As Lord King): Lady Renounce, if you don't get rid of her, you better send her back to the Development Group or at least keep her away from me. Not only was the content garbage, but the format she used is ten years out of date.

R : (As LR): I'll rein her in your majesty. My deepest apologies.

J : (As Lord King): Just get me that report to me by midnight.

R : (As LR): Absolutely, your highness.

J : Isn't Lady Renounce being just a bit unethical?

R : It's called *Miz-Management* Jimmy. Now there's another note to read.

J : OK. LR checks her e-mail and forwards a copy of Cinderella's report to Azmella. She then yells for Azmella to come into her office.

R : So I'm LR again, Jimmy. (As LR): Azmella, I need you to reformat Cinderella's report, because it's a mess. Your sister will also need to edit it for grammar and spelling. E-mail it to me when you're finished, so I can check it over carefully before at midnight.

J : Who turns into a pumpkin?

R : Nobody, Jimmy.

J : Am I *Azmella* again?

R : Aye, Jimmy, you are.

J : (As A): But Mommy, it's after three already and it will take at least a three hours to finish this.

R : (As LR): Just do the best you can my dearest. I have to go now.

J : Wow. Mommy is very popular with everyone isn't she?

R : Brilliant, Jimmy. Read the next note.

J : This is a long skit Red.

R : It would be shorter if you'd stop interrupting, Jimmy.

J : Fine. Azmella e-mails the finished copy to Mommy at 7:35. LR has a quick look at it, inserts her own name in the "prepared by" section and heads off to her bridge game. After returning from her bridge game, she watches the news and forwards an e-mail copy of the draft report to Lord King at 11:00 PM. LR shows up with the final printed report at the palace uncharacteristically on time (before midnight).

R : (As LR): Greetings your majesty.

J : (As Lord King): Ah, Lady Renounce. Great job on that IAR. You always come through for me.

R : (As LR): Thank you your highness, I do my best.

J : Wait just a minute, Red. Don't tell me that this skit was based on a real situation.

R : Did I say that, Jimmy?

J : Well no, but surely real people don't behave like this today?

R : That's why we're writing this book, Jimmy. Y'see, there are a lot of *Miz-Managers* out there who are excellent at *Dumb-ping* and even at *Losing* stuff, but they don't know how to take that extra step, the way Lady Renounce did.

J : So what happened to the glass slippers?

R : Don't be ridiculous, Jimmy. Nobody's stu-pid enough to wear slippers made of glass.

J : Not even a Mizzy?

R : No, Jimmy, not even a Mizzy.

J : No doubt Lady Renounce's family lives in a very effective Miz-Envi-ronment, but I noticed she didn't even try to influence the King.

R : No point, Jimmy.

J : Why not?

R : Because she rarely spends any time at the palace, and she needs the King's support to keep her job. This allows her to continue to develop a highly effective *Miz-Environment* in her own area.

J : Seems like a missed opportunity.

R : Not at all, Jimmy. Lord King is also a *Mizzy* and most parasites don't kill their hosts.

J : Maybe not, but I feel like I just killed a perfectly good day.

R : It's not over yet, Jimmy. It's only 4 o'clock.

J : Great. I can go play Bridge and then work on the book until midnight.

R : Send me a copy when you're finished, prefer-ably before midnight then, Jimmy.

J : Are we done then?

R : We are, Jimmy. At least that pretty much wraps up Chapter 25 anyway.

J : And the next Chapter is still 24?

R : Right on, Jimmy. Same time on Saturday? Let's meet at the Second Cup in the Library. Coffee's on me.

J : OK…

By the time the 'K' rolled off my tongue, Red had already reached the escalator in Telus Plaza. It wouldn't have mattered what I said, for he had already determined that the answer would be yes.

I still had this nagging feeling that I was being set up, but I had to admit that, if nothing else, Red was both interesting and entertaining. I couldn't help but wonder if there really were people out there who behaved like Lady Renounce. Was I being naïve to think that people in senior management positions could never be that unethical, and was Red just exaggerating for the sake of effect? It was perplexing.

I still had a lot of unanswered questions, but as I scanned through my notes I could see some potential in the material I was collecting from Red. Maybe—just maybe—there was something workable in all this. Feeling slightly optimistic for the first time in weeks, I headed home a little bewildered, but with some degree of hope.

CHAPTER 24

THE TERGIVERSATOR
(JUMPER)

FU
RETURN
[THE TURNING POINT]

Tergiversate

To change one's mind, subterfuge, to use evasions or ambiguities, to change sides, to turn back

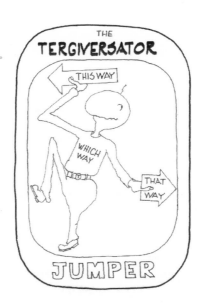

During my five-day break from Red, I found time to reflect on Red's skit and to read through my notes several times. The more I analyzed the '*wisdom*' of Red Knech, the less preposterous his reckonings seemed to be; however, the behaviour of Lady Renounce in the skit was still nagging me with curiosity as to whether or not it was pure fiction or fact-based. Acutely aware of the social significance of either being affiliated with, or promoting, the curious reckonings of Mr. Ephred Knech, I found myself wondering if I might inadvertently be heading down the proverbial path to Ponoka.

For those who may not be familiar with that name, Ponoka is a small town nestled in heart of central Alberta, just off the Calgary/Edmonton corridor known as QE II. It is perhaps best known for the Ponoka Stampede and its Psychiatric Facilities at Alberta Hospital Ponoka. Not being a staunch rodeo fan, I found my mind drifting back to an article that I had recently read about life in the Brain Injury Unit at Ponoka, but a most fortunate reality check jolted me back to the present with the realization that I had just sauntered right past Second Cup.

For a brief moment, I stopped and stared straight ahead toward my subconscious destination. As I gazed into the distant landscape, southward across the North Saskatchewan River, I was visualizing a future in Ponoka. Of course, I couldn't see anything as far as 100 Kilometres away, but I knew it was there, calling me, and I was subconsciously heading straight for it. I'm sure that Dr. Freud would have had an interesting theory on that thought.

Ready or not, it was time for yet another session with the inimitable Mr. Red Knech, so I turned back and headed for the café. As I entered the Second Cup, I was surprised to see that there was no sign of Red anywhere. What a quandary!

However, I figured that since I was here anyway, I might as well join the line for my afternoon coffee fix. As I stood there, contemplating the menu board behind the counter, I dropped my leather notebook when a hand surprisingly slapped me on my shoulder.

R : I thought you weren't coming in then, Jimmy.
J : Oh Red, it's you. You scared me. I didn't see you.
R : I went to the wee laddie's room when I thought you weren't coming in.
J : I'm only a couple of minutes late.
R : Aye, Jimmy, but I noticed that you walked right by the door there, and it seemed like you were heading off somewhere else.
J : Sorry, I've never been in this Second Cup before and I had a lot on my mind, so I missed the entrance.
R : Thinking about our book, were ya, Jimmy?
J : Not really.
R : What then, Jimmy?
J : Well, if you really want to know, I was thinking about a… rodeo?
R : No, Jimmy, the young lady behind the counter wants to know what you'll be having to drink then.

J :   Oh, sorry.

R :   Don't forget, Jimmy, I'm buying this time.

J :   Great! I'll have a medium paradiso and a cranberry muffin thanks.

R :   It's not lunch, Jimmy.

J :   Oh, Sorry! OK, just the coffee will be fine thanks.

R :   There y'go laddie, one small dark.

J :   Thanks a lot, Red.

R :   No problem, Jimmy. So which one was it?

J :   I think we were finished with the Abdicator and the next one should be the Tergiversator, according to my notes.

R :   Not that, Jimmy, which Rodeo were you thinking about?

J :   Does it matter?

R :   It does, Jimmy.

J :   Irregardless of which one, the point is that it's a rodeo.

R :   Wrong, Jimmy.

J :   Why is it wrong?

R :   It's not a real word, Jimmy.

J :   Rodeo is definitely a real word, Red. I know they don't have them in Scot…

R :   Not Rodeo, Jimmy. Irregardless… it's not in the dictionary.

J :   Well, a lot of people use it… and look who's talking.

R :   Just because others use it wrong, Jimmy, doesn't make it right for you to use it wrong in our book. You can use regardless, or irrespective, for example. Those are real words.

J :   OK, fine. Well actually, I was thinking about the Ponoka Stampede. Are you a rodeo fan?

R :   Not at all, Jimmy.

J :   Have you ever been to a rodeo?

R :   Once a year, Jimmy.

J :   You go every year?

R :   Aye, Jimmy, I do.

J :   But I thought you said you weren't a rodeo fan.

R :   I'm not, Jimmy. Can't really stand them.

J :   Then why do you go?

R :   I used to be a *Maxi-Mizzy* myself, Jimmy. But since coming to Alberta I've become reformed.

J :   You do know that the Reform Party merged with the Conservatives, so it's unlikely you really are a Reformer?

R :   Not politics, Jimmy, it's me. I've reformed, and now I'm only a *Mini-Mizzy*.

J :   Which means?

R :   Being reformed, Jimmy, I only need a wee bit of *Miz-Adventure* in my life to satisfy all my *Miz-Needs*.

J :   And a rodeo does that for you?

R :   It does indeed, Jimmy, especially the Ponoka Stampede.

J :   You go to Ponoka once a year?

R : I do, Jimmy.

J : What's so special for you about the rodeo in Ponoka?

R : It's in Ponoka, Jimmy.

J : Does that mean you like Ponoka or you don't?

R : It's a brilliant wee town, Jimmy.

J : Brilliant again? So what makes it so brilliant?

R : Ponoka, Jimmy, is the perfect location for two important functions; a rodeo and a Loonie Bin.

J : You mean a psychiatric hospital.

R : Are we being politically correct then, Jimmy?

J : Don't you think that the word *'Loonie Bin'* is a bit derogatory for the patients who live there?

R : Did I say anything about the patients, Jimmy?

J : Let's not go there. I suppose you want me to ask you why it's the perfect location.

R : Good question, Jimmy. Well for starters, it's the centre of the universe.

J : You know, Red; I'm not even going respond to that one.

R : Good plan, Jimmy. Another reason is that, for a Stampede, it's hard to find a better site.

J : OK, I'll give you that, and for a psychiatric hospital?

R : Out of mind, out of sight, Jimmy.

J : OK, let's not go there either.

R : You should go, Jimmy. You'd like Ponoka.

J : I didn't mean… never mind. You go to Ponoka every year then?

R : Every year, Jimmy. Wouldn't miss it.

J : But you don't really enjoy it?

R : Not so much the rodeo, Jimmy, but I do enjoy the people. They're brilliant.

J : Brilliant good?

R : Aye, Jimmy, they're very interesting indeed. I've always felt a wee bit of jealousy toward people who can be so incredibly passionate about an activity that serves no really useful purpose.

J : I expect that most rodeo fans might challenge your reckoning on the point of *'no useful purpose'*.

R : They might indeed, Jimmy. As would golfers, curlers, hunters, paintball players, video game enthusiasts, and a myriad of others who have an addictive passion for such un-purposeful activities.

J : You know Red, these types of activities are a very important part of the lives of a lot of people, and not just here in Alberta.

R : They are indeed, Jimmy. I didn't say they weren't important, just not very purposeful.

J : Don't any of your friends participate in these types of recreational activities?

R : Aye, they do, Jimmy.

J : But you don't?

R : Not anymore, Jimmy.

J : Is that because they aren't productive or because you don't enjoy them?

R : Neither, Jimmy. It's because I'm not really very good at them, and since my *Miz-Addictions* have declined a lot in my old age, I don't have the same need to fulfill my *Humiliation Factor* anymore.

J : Are we going to discuss the humiliation factor then?

R : In Chapter 27, Jimmy.

J : OK, no rush. Aren't you interested in any types of physical fitness or recreation?

R : That's the last thing I'd be interested in, Jimmy.

J : Of course it's none of my business, but… since you mentioned your age, don't you think you should consider doing some kind of exercise to keep fit.

R : I do, Jimmy.

J : I thought you said you weren't interested?

R : No Jimmy. I said that'll be last.

J : Last what?

R : The last book, Jimmy. Pay attention. That'll be the last book in the series.

J : You mean Book VIII?

R : No Jimmy, Book VII. Book VIII will be the third book released in the series.

J : Oh! So Book VII is going to be the last book to be released. Is that it?

R : Aye, Jimmy. Now stay with me, if y'can.

J : I'm trying.

R : You are that Jimmy.

J : Touché. Is Book VII about recreation?

R : No it's about fitness, Jimmy.

J : Sorry. I get confused. I guess that was just another brilliant question.

R : Not at all, Jimmy. We'll get to recreation in book IV.

J : Is that the next book you'll be working on, or would it be too much to expect Book IV to follow Book III?

R : It would Jimmy. Book V will be the next one you write.

J : I will write?

R : Maybe Jimmy. If y'do a good job on this one.

J : Great! I can hardly wait. But maybe right now we should get back to Book III?

R : Good plan, Jimmy.

J : Just one question before we start on Chapter 24.

R : What's that then, Jimmy?

J : That last skit about Dumbper the Abdicator… Was that really based on a real incident?

R : Did I say that, Jimmy?

J : No, not really.

R : Did I ever suggest this was anything but fiction, Jimmy?

J : No.

R :   Well, there's your answer then, Jimmy.

J :   That's not an answer; that's evasion.

R :   Well it's all you're going to get, Laddie. If we say it's fabricated, we lose credibility, and if we say it's true, we could face a lawsuit.

J :   What do you mean *we*?

R :   Your name will be on the cover, Jimmy.

J :   OK then. Let's go to the next chapter. Could you tell me a bit about this Tergiversator?

R :   Just like a chameleon, Jimmy, the *Tergiversator* is always changing.

J :   In what way?

R :   Metaphorically speaking, Jimmy.

J :   I kind of assumed that it wouldn't be a physical change, like a real chameleon.

R :   Brilliant assumption, Jimmy. Remember; *Exasperation, Annoyance* and *Frustration* are three of the foundation stones for creating an effective *Miz-Environment*.

J :   And change fosters these factors?

R :   It does, Jimmy, but it's not change in general that does it. It's focused change.

J :   Focused on what?

R :   Transformation, Jimmy. Change that generates *Stress, Depression,* and *Alienation.*

J :   How do we do that?

R :   Practice, Jimmy.

J :   Right, so what are we practicing this time?

R :   R-A-T, Jimmy.

J :   Rats? Did you say rat?

R :   Running rampant everywhere, Jimmy.

J :   Here in Second Cup? I don't see any evidence of rats around here.

R :   There may be some evidence around here, Jimmy, but it's often hard to tell unless you get behind the scenes so to speak.

J :   No… no… hang on a minute there, Red, you are definitely wrong. There are no rats in Alberta, except maybe at the University labs. That's something that we're very proud of in this province.

R :   What are you on about now, Jimmy?

J :   They even had a TV show about rats. I think it was called the Rat Patrol or something—

R :   Are you deaf and daft, Jimmy? I'm trying to explain the behavioural practices of *Reorganizing, Adjusting* and *Transforming* and you're off on some other tangent about rats.

J :   But you just spelled out R-A-T and—

R :   And you jumped to another conclusion. Do y'have a thing about rats then, Jimmy?

J :   No, I… never mind. OK, so I misunderstood. Do I take it that the 'R' stands for *Reorganizing,* the 'A' for *Adjusting* and the 'T' for *Transforming*?

R : That's what I just said, Jimmy.

J : Those types of changes can definitely be stress-ful. Can you provide some examples?

R : Well Jimmy, there's *Fluctuation* and *Vacillation*.

J : Aren't they the same?

R : Not at all, Jimmy. *Fluctuation* is constant change and *Vacillation* is wavering.

J : Sort of like change on steroids?

R : Perpetual change management, Jimmy. That's exactly the kind of atmosphere that *Jumper* wants to create.

J : *Jumper*? Are we talking about a horse or a seal or something?

R : No, Jimmy. Did you forget about the Latin names and common names?

J : I did forget. Is *Jumper* the common name for *Tergiversator*, like *Dumbper* is for *Abdicator*?

R : Good guess, Jimmy.

J : So would the *Tergiversator's* job be to perpetu-ate a constant state of change?

R : It would indeed, Jimmy. It seems I don't have to tell you anything anymore.

J : I wish.

R : Wish what, Jimmy?

J : Nothing! OK, let's start with the first one. How does the *Tergiversator* practice *Reorganizing* to perpetuate change?

R : Have you ever played the game of musical chairs, Jimmy?

J : Sure, hasn't everyone?

R : Great, Jimmy. What do people do when they play musical chairs?

J : They dance around to the music until it stops, and then they try to sit down on one of the chairs before someone else does.

R : Exactly, Jimmy. Do you think it would be possible to get any work done if you were playing musical chairs all the time?

J : Of course not, but why would you be play-ing a game when there's work to be done?

R : Why indeed, Jimmy? Unless it's golf, but that's another story al-together. So, if *Jumper* can keep the workplace in a perpetual state of *Reorganization*, it's a lot like playing musical chairs at work.

J : How so?

R : Y'see Jimmy, if you are always *Reorganizing*, everyone will always be either dancing around trying to keep their jobs by making sure that others look bad or by vying for one of the other jobs up for grabs.

J : It does sound a bit like playing musical chairs.

R : Just so, Jimmy. That means they'll be so busy rearranging meet-ings, calling union meetings, checking out which jobs are being posted, writing resumes, filling out applications, going to inter-views, bad mouthing their colleagues, and most important, worrying about the future, that they will actually never get anything done.

J : Sounds like chaos.

R : It's *Disruptive,* Jimmy.

J : Aren't they similar?

R : They are, Jimmy, but, while chaos means constant disorder with no hope for improvement, *Disruptive* pretends to be correcting the problems associated with chaos.

J : What difference does that make?

R : In an environment of chaos, many people choose to leave, but in a *Disruptive Miz-Environment,* people have the hope of improvement and they will stay and work in constant *Mizery.*

J : But there is no real chance for improvement, right?

R : Brilliant, Jimmy. *Jumper's* long term objective is to create a constant *Disruptive Miz-Environment.*

J : Now it sounds stressful.

R : Doesn't it just, Jimmy. *Stress* can contribute so much to creating an effective *Miz-Environment.* It also means that people who are competing with each other are constantly guarded and uncooperative, which is another key ingredient to undermining effective teamwork.

J : There are a lot of good books out there that support change as being not only positive, but also necessary to keep pace with the times.

R : That's the beauty of it, Jimmy. You can use those books to champion your cause and defend the need for change.

J : But, isn't change sometimes a good thing?

R : Depends on your perspective, Jimmy. Sometimes it is, but sometimes it's not. When people are hoping for change and a plan is developed, sometimes the actual changes can be very disappointing if they don't meet people's expectations, unless of course they are *Mizzies.*

J : For example?

R : Like the old Soviet Army underwear joke, Jimmy.

J : The what?

R : Do y'not know that joke them, Jimmy? You're probably too young.

J : Somehow, I think I'm going to regret this, but … go ahead, let's hear it.

R : Back during the cold war, Jimmy, the Soviet Army was very large indeed, and they required a lot of warm clothes. At one point when underwear was in very short supply, the soldiers were getting quite concerned.

J : I imagine they would be, *especially* in Siberia during the winter.

R : Being as you're from Winnipeg, Jimmy, y'can probably appreciate that then.

J : I guess I walked into that one. So did the soldiers get new underwear?

R : It was announced, Jimmy, that they would all get a change of underwear.

J : Change is good. So they got new underwear?

R : No, Jimmy, they got a change of underwear. Boris changed with Ivan and Igor changed with Vladimir, and so on and so forth.

J : Whoa there Red! You can't use that kind of material in a book; it's politically incorrect and disrespectful to our friends in Russia.

R : It didn't used to be, Jimmy.

J : Well maybe it wasn't back in the Stone Age, when you were young, but it should have been even then, and it definitely is not acceptable today.

R : No problem. Jimmy, just change '*Soviet*' to '*Taliban*,' that should do it.

J : C'mon, Red, let's get serious here.

R : We could change it to diapers, Jimmy. That way they'd each have to learn to live with someone else's shi... ah... faeces.

J : That's enough, Red. Remember, you said it's a family book. Why would you want to include something like that in a book anyway?

R : Because I'm sick of hearing about the boiled frog, Jimmy. It's been overdone to death—pun intended.

J : You're right about that, Red. My profs use it a lot, whenever the subject of change management is being discussed.

R : It's actually a great one, Jimmy, for encouraging people to get on the change bandwagon, but even though it still provides a modicum of annoyance for me, I've had enough.

J : Me too. Now, you were saying that sometimes change is good and sometimes it's not. Do you always want them to get on the bandwagon?

R : Not really, Jimmy, unless it's change that is either unnecessary or not beneficial.

J : Who's going to support change that's not beneficial?

R : P^{3}s, Jimmy, and *Mizzies,* of course. Most of them never really look at the proposals for change or think it through, but they are so anxious to be seen as progressive transformers, that they'll likely approve any proposed change, no matter how ill-conceived it may be.

J : But, as you said, sometimes change is actually good, and you can't always stop positive change from happening.

R : Fortunately, most changes within any large existing organization take a long time to materialize and aren't usually that beneficial.

J : That's not what they teach us in the business program.

R : That's great for *Mizzies,* Jimmy, but can you think of any good examples?

J : What about the Post Office, where you work? They've gone through enormous changes over the years and hasn't it improved service?

R : I must have missed that one, Jimmy. Do you mean the service of fifty years ago, when real mail was delivered right to your door, as compared to the ton of junk mail delivered to some group box in your neighbourhood today?

J : My group box is on the main floor of my apartment building.

R : Good for you, Jimmy, but in the suburbs, it's a place you have to walk to in the rain, sleet and snow just so you can retrieve junk mail and throw it in the recycle bin?

J : It's not that bad.

R : Actually you're right, Jimmy; it's an excellent example of improvement—for *Mizzies.*

J : Well, at least you get some exercise.

R : Even the best changes aren't always perfect, Jimmy.

J : So, are you advocating only non-beneficial change?

R : Just any change for the sake of change, Jimmy.

J : Why is that different?

R : It's constant, Jimmy.

J : Isn't there a saying that the only constant is change?

R : Comes from ancient China, Jimmy.

J : Like your book on the *I Ching*?

R : Not really, Jimmy, even though the I Ch-ing is also known as the Book of Change.

J : So is constant change good?

R : For the *Miz-Manager,* Jimmy, constant change is always effective.

J : So, if constant change is good for creating a Miz-Environment, what type of changes might the Tergiversator introduce to disrupt the working environment, aside from underwear and frogs?

R : It doesn't really matter, Jimmy, as long as it's perpetual and ineffective.

J : Isn't perpetual change the same as constant change?

R : Not quite, Jimmy. Constant is continuous, and per-petual is continually repeated.

J : Great, we could start a "Change-of-the-month' club?

R : That's a grand idea, Jimmy. Perpetual reorganization is always very disruptive and has proven to be a very effective method for contaminating and demoralizing the work environment.

J : Maybe so, but what organization would ever sup-port perpetually reorganization?

R : Aside from governments and public institutions, who do it all the time, you'd be surprised, Jimmy. *Brillies,* however, would never publicly or intentionally support perpetual reorganiza-tion, unless they were convinced that it was necessary.

J : So what makes it necessary?

R : It's not necessary, Jimmy.

J : But you just said it *was* necessary.

R : The key words are 'convinced' and 'intentional,' Jimmy, not nec-essary. If the *Miz-Manager* is the only one who knows it's in-tentional and can convince her P^3 bosses that it's a good idea, then it's not really intentional or necessary is it?

J : How does the Miz-Manager convince any-one that change is necessary then?

R : Senior management is usually ready to support any change, so if *Jumper* says it's necessary, then it must be necessary, right Jimmy?

J : What if someone figures it out that it's not really necessary?

R : Well if they do, Jimmy, then *Jumper* simply makes sure they don't get a chair when the music stops.

J : Even if it is effective, it sounds like a lot of work.

R : Not at all, Jimmy. *Miz-Managers* simply have to put on their *Dumbper* hats and dumbp it on someone else or engage the support of their unions.

J : Of course! I was just about to suggest that, but how can the unions help?

R : First of all, Jimmy, it's important to either have more than one union in your company or reorganize the union structure to have at least two unions if you want them to contribute to your *Disruptive Miz-Environment*.

J : Why would you have more than one union?

R : It promotes inequity, Jimmy, and provides opportunities for conflict between the unions.

J : For example?

R : On a really large construction site, Jimmy, there are always several unions, and if a member of one union *Alienates* a member of another union, the results can be most auspicious.

J : In what way?

R : Relieving is one way, Jimmy.

J : Relieving someone on another shift or what?

R : No. No, Jimmy. Take the situation where a steelworker is 10 storeys up, and there are no Porta Pottys up that high.

J : So?

R : He's had a lot to drink Jimmy, use your imagination.

J : So what?

R : Still a bit slow, Jimmy? He relieves himself and fortunately, there's a member of the Carpenter Union directly below.

J : That's disgusting.

R : Very disgusting indeed, Jimmy. So the Carpenter Union complains and the Steelworker gets fired.

J : Deservedly, I'd say.

R : Not if you're a Steelworker, Jimmy. So the Steelworkers walk.

J : Really?

R : Then management gets involved, because a strike costs them a million dollars a day, and they agree to rehire a member of the Steelworker's Union.

J : Well, I suppose they need a replacement.

R : Except, Jimmy, the Steelworkers want the right to pick the replacement worker.

J : Sounds fair enough.

R : Not to the Carpenters Union, Jimmy.

J : Why not?

R : Because, Jimmy, the Steelworker Union picked the same guy that just got fired, so all the Carpenters walk.

J : A lot of walking going on.

R : Not really much walking, Jimmy, but lots of drinking as both unions head off to the bar together to enjoy a 3 or 4 day break.

J : Well that doesn't sound so miserable.

R : Maybe not for the workers at the bar, Jimmy, but it costs management a lot.

J : OK, I guess that's miserable for management.

R : And *Disruptive* for sure, Jimmy.

J : So now I think we've covered the Reorganizing, what about Adjusting?

R : Did your mother ever say to y'Jimmy, "Don't get too comfortable now?"

J : Sounds a bit familiar.

R : And what did she mean, Jimmy?

J : Usually it meant she had some stupid job for me to do.

R : Exactly, Jimmy. And how did that make you feel?

J : Uncomfortable?

R : There y'go, Jimmy. People who feel uncomfortable all the time can make a significant contribution towards creating an effective *Miz-Environment*, just like P³s.

J : What do P³s have to do with being uncomfortable?

R : Well Jimmy, Dr. Peter called them incompetent, which is evident by their behaviour, but in many cases their judgement was simply impaired because they felt so uncomfortable.

J : This may be true, but you can't just go up to people and say, "Don't get too comfortable."

R : Of course not, Jimmy. That's why *Jumper* has to learn to make good use of her limited time and infrequent visits to the office.

J : Are you suggesting that people who feel uncomfortable don't come to work very often?

R : Aye, Jimmy, especially *Tergiversators.* They usually try not to be around very much, which is why they have to use their time wisely to find out who is comfortable in their jobs.

J : Wait a minute, why aren't *Tergiversators* around very much? Don't they have to be in the office to experience the wonderful *Miz-Environment* that they have created?

R : They would, Jimmy, if their workplace really was an effective *Miz-Environment,* but most aren't. This is why they stay away and why we are writing this book.

J : If they are rarely in the office, how can they tell who's comfortable?

R : Detective work, Jimmy. Like **Hercule Poirot,** they just have to look around the workplace and see who is smiling, who has happy face stickers at their desk, and who is really enjoying their work. They should also check out the productivity figures and find out if anyone is receiving positive feedback from clients. They'll soon know who's guilty of being too comfortable.

J : Then what?

R : Then, Jimmy, *Jumper* issues instructions to staff to adjust what they are doing.

J : Adjust to what?

R : Anything that makes them uncomfortable, Jimmy.

J : That's really not very helpful Red. Maybe we should move on to *Transforming*? What's so special about *Transforming*?

R : It's dramatic, Jimmy.

J : Dramatic in what way?

R : Two ways, Jimmy. The first is a major transformation at a personal level, and the second is much bigger at the corporate level.

J : So just because something is major or big, does that make it dramatic?

R : Aye, Jimmy, it does.

J : Ok, I'm listening.

R : There's listening, and then there's understanding, Jimmy.

J : Right, and at this moment, I understand that I need a break.

R : Good idea, Jimmy. I think it's your turn to buy.

J : OK. What'll you have?

R : Same as always, Jimmy.
Standing in long line-ups used to annoy me a lot, but perhaps because it was such a relief to break from the reckonings of Red Knech, I actually enjoyed the wait.

J : Here you go, Red. Did I get it right?

R : Brilliant, Jimmy. Thanks very much.

J : So where were we?

R : Transforming, Jimmy.

J : Right; at the personal and corporate levels. Can you please help me understand what a personal transformation is?

R : Attitude adjustment there, Jimmy.

J : I said, please. What more do you want?

R : Not *your* attitude, Jimmy. Although I thought I detected a wee bit of *Frustration* in your voice.

J : Whose attitude then? And I'm *not* frustrated, maybe just a bit tired.

R : Tired of what, Jimmy? You don't do much all day but drink coffee.

J : I'm probably transforming into a caffeine addict or worse, a *Mizzie*.

R : That's the spirit, Jimmy. *Pessimism*.

J : I'll adjust.

R : No, it's perfect, Jimmy. You've just demonstrated how an attitude adjustment toward *Pessimism* can transform enthusiasm to cynicism.

J : It wasn't intentional.

R : It doesn't matter, Jimmy. Y'see, personal transformation is fundamentally an attitude adjustment and *Jumper* has to master *Capricious Pessimism*.

J : Like turning people into Zombies?

R : Good one, Jimmy. Zombies may be a bit extreme, but people with similar attitudes can really enhance your *Miz-Environment*.

J : I suppose that the *Brillies* will be trying to counter *Jumper's* efforts by promoting positive attitude adjustments.

R : You suppose correctly, Jimmy, but fortunately it's much easier to transform to *Pessimism* than to convert to *Optimism*.

J : What about that 'infectious enthusiasm' that you talked about earlier?

R : Did you really remember that by yourself, Jimmy, or did you cheat and read from your notes?

J : I have a very good memory. I can even remember a lot of nonsense.

R : I think you've got it, Jimmy.

J : Got what?

R : Perfidious Negativism, Jimmy.

J : Really? It's that bad?

R : It's brilliant for *Dumbper*, Jimmy. Do y'see how easy it is to incite *Negativism* in someone else?

J : If you mean me, it's working.

R : Great, Jimmy. Y'see a lot of it in the workplace. First it starts with gossip mongering, which usually leads to whining and complaining. Then, if properly managed, it can escalate to scepticism, which typically generates a lot of sarcasm, and before you know it, the people around you are transformed into the cynics that you need to help build an effective *Miz-Environment*.

J : Wouldn't it be easier to just say that infectious cynicism means getting everyone pis—

R : Uh uh, Jimmy, you can't use that kind of language.

J : OK, *ticked off* then?

R : No, you're confusing the objective with the process.

J : You have a special process for pis— sorry, ticking people off?

R : Of course, Jimmy.

J : What a surprise.

R : That's it exactly, Jimmy.

J : It's a surprise?

R : Don't be daft, Jimmy. It's your attitude and behaviour that ticks people off… and that's no surprise.

J : My attitude?

R : Aye, Jimmy, especially those cynical and sarcastic comments you're always making.

J : Sorry, I suppose I may have been a little insensitive.

R : Not at all, Jimmy. You exemplify the process perfectly.

J : What process?

R : The process that generates *Vacillation* and *Fluctuation*, Jimmy, or as you would say it; *'the process to piss people off.'*

J : Hold on Red! You just said I couldn't use that word.

R : Not in the book, Jimmy.

J : Well?

R : I didn't say I couldn't use it, Jimmy.

J : Right. The proverbial double standard. And now it's my process?

R : Definitely, Jimmy, after all, what are you really trying to do when you behave with scepticism, cynicism, and sarcasm?

J : Be funny?

R : C'mon, Jimmy. You know you wouldn't last ten seconds at Yuk Yuks.

J : I suppose you're right. Too much scepticism, cynicism, and sarcasm in the workplace could be a bit disruptive.

R : Absolutely, Jimmy. A *Miz-mm* attitude is what the *Miz-*

Manager must strive to achieve in the workplace.

J :   A *Miz-mm* attitude?

R :   Careful, Jimmy, you're repeating again.

J :   Sorry, Red, I know you mentioned it in the last chapter, but I must have missed the definition for '*Miz-mm* attitude.'

R :   Y'said it yourself, Jimmy: *Scepticism, Cynicism,* and *Sarcasm.*

J :   I see, negative words that end with an elongated '*m.*'

R :   Brilliant, Jimmy. Any sign of *Miz-mms* in the workplace is a sign of progress.

J :   Like scepticism, cynicism, and sarcasm?

R :   We're not limited to those three, Jimmy. Sardonicism, Pessimism, Nihilism, Negativism, Anarchism, and Syndicalism are also signs of progressive Miz-mms.

J :   Syndicalism?

R :   It's probably not in your wee dictionary, Jimmy, so I'll help you out. It's like the tail wagging the dog.

J :   What's that mean?

R :   It's like when the unions take over running the business into the ground, Jimmy. They have even less understanding of business than managers, so whenever they take over, Miz-Progress is bound to follow.

J :   Like what you do then?

R :   Don't get personal, Jimmy; I'm not a *Maxi-Mizzy.*

J :   Right.

R :   Y'see Jimmy, behaviour drives the change process, and attitude fuels behaviour, so it's important to transform people's attitudes to be more negative—like yours.

J :   Like mine?

R :   Aye, Jimmy, full of Sarcasm, Scepticism, and Cynicism.

J :   I'm not always like that.

R :   That's a shame, Jimmy, but true. Sometimes you're obnoxious, insufferable, irritating, and exasperating.

J :   Well don't stop now, you're just getting started.

R :   No, that's quite enough, Jimmy.

J :   What's stopping you?

R :   I don't know you that well, Jimmy.

J :   Ok! Thanks, Red. I think you've clearly demonstrated the process for how to transform a positive attitude into a negative attitude.

R :   You're a fast learner, Jimmy, and you do have a brilliant *Miz-mm* attitude, which is necessary to counter *Ubiquitous Optimism.*

J :   Ubiquitous optimism? Oh good, more obscure words?

R :   Do you need to check your wee dictionary then, Jimmy?

J :   No!

R :   Y'see Jimmy, just like *Infectious Enthusiasm* is the nemesis for the *Abdicator, Ubiquitous Optimism* is the antagonist for the *Tergiversator.*

J :   So what you're saying is that Miz-mms can counter the effects of ubiquitous optimism?

R : Indeed, Jimmy, but to initiate sufficient *Miz-mms* in the workplace, first you must practice *Reorganizing, Adjusting, and Transforming* to *Stress, Depress,* and *Alienate* people so they will a develop a *Miz-mm* attitude.

J : And this will counter the behaviour of those ubiquitous optimistic Brillies?

R : No, Jimmy, it simply destabilizes their *Dependability and Sincerity.*

J : Rats!

R : Exactly, Jimmy. Practicing the RAT process, which—

J : No, I meant rats, now there are two more new words to contend with.

R : *Dependability* and *Sincerity* aren't new words, Jimmy; they're just not very commonly practiced.

J : So why mention them?

R : Because, Jimmy, they are the behaviours of the *Tergiversator's* nemesis.

J : Ubiquitous optimism again?

R : That's the attitude, Jimmy.

J : Now you think I'm ubiquitous and optimistic?

R : No, Jimmy. That's the attitude of *Jumper's* nemesis.

J : Oh, *those* guys.

R : Aye, Jimmy. Y'know, the dependable and sincere Brillies who're determined to *Develop* a workplace that is *Progressive* in a highly *Productive* environment.

J : Good thing they aren't very common then, I guess?

R : Y'guess right there, Jimmy. They're always running around sticking their noses in other people's business trying to help them out and show them ways of improving themselves, their skills and their knowledge.

J : You mean the 'Go To' people who actually know how things work and how to get things done?

R : That's them, Jimmy.

J : Well, we can't have that, can we?

R : No we can't, Jimmy.

J : I think that pretty much covers personal transformation for me, so what about corporate transformation?

R : That's the big one, Jimmy. Unfortunately, unless the *Tergiversator* is at a very senior level, it's usually very difficult to initiate *Transformation* at the corporate level.

J : What kind of transformation are we talking about?

R : Major *Transformation,* Jimmy. A good example would be IBM.

J : But IBM is still going strong today.

R : True, Jimmy, but if you think back to the eighties, their business was predominantly manufacturing computers and hardware.

J : So?

R : Well today, Jimmy, probably three quarters of their business is in the field of management of systems and consulting. That was a major transformation.

J :   That's pretty major all right. Any others?

R :   The Swiss watchmakers, Jimmy. Before digital battery watches, the Swiss were the best watchmakers in the world.

J :   Aren't they still?

R :   Because they transformed, Jimmy.

J :   How?

R :   Back then, Jimmy, along came the Japanese with their battery operated digital watches like Seiko.

J :   But wouldn't you call that a paradigm shift?

R :   Call it what you like, Jimmy, its still *Transformation*.

J :   OK, so let me get this straight… the RAT practices are used to introduce constant change by *Reorganizing* to generate *Stress; Adjusting* to cause *Depression* and *Transforming* to *Alienate* people, is that it?

R :   Amazing, Jimmy! I didn't really think you were listening.

J :   Bibbidi-Bobbidi-Boo and what do we get?

R :   A Disruptive Miz-Environnent, Jimmy.

J :   Full of *Miz-mms*?

R :   Bingo, Jimmy.

J :   OK, let's see if I can get three in a row. Correct me if I'm wrong— and I'm sure you will—but all *Jumper* really needs to do, to counter the positive attitudes of these ubiquitous, optimistic Brillies, is simply practice being a RAT to generate a sufficient amount of *Stress, Depression,* and *Alienation* in the workplace to create a *Disruptive* environment where *Fluctuation* and *Vacillation* can flourish in an atmosphere of *Miz-mms*. Does that about sum it up?

R :   Almost, but not quite, Jimmy.

J :   Rats! There goes my winning streak. I suppose that means I won't get my *Tergiversator* certificate?

R :   Not RATs Jimmy—*Checking*.

J :   What are you checking for now?

R :   Penalties, Jimmy.

J :   Ah, checking, like another hockey penalty?

R :   Aye Jimmy, one for RATs

J :   Got it, but somehow I thought it would be tripping for *Jumper*.

R :   *Tripping* is for the *Equivocator* Jimmy, *Checking* is for Jumper.

J :   OK. And Checking means hitting an opponent from behind.

R :   You seem to know your penalties there, Jimmy.

J :   I know that one. So we now have another hockey penalty to add to the list.

R :   Exactly, Jimmy. The RAT practices are known to *Mizzies* as *Checking* because of the similarity of their effectiveness both on the ice and in the workplace.

J :   Except there's no penalty in the workplace, right?

R :   Right, Jimmy. You do have a memory. Once you have established an effective *Miz-Environment*, you have to maintain it by keeping it in check.

J :   So… checking means that *Jumper* is an effective RAT?

R : She might be, Jimmy, if she earns the *Distrust* of her staff to
be referred to as being *Unreliable* and *Unpredictable*.

J : Something to really strive for all right. How does one
go about achieving such an enviable reputation?

R : A reputation of *Distrust* has to be earned, Jimmy, through attitude
adjustment, behaviour modification, and by practicing *Checking*.

J : Of course it does, but that could be really tough for our hero.

R : Not really, Jimmy. She simply starts by being *Undependable*
and *Disingenuous,* and the rest will follow quite naturally.

J : That's it? I had no idea it could be that easy.

R : Are y'keeping good notes there, Jimmy?

J : Don't you trust me then?

R : I do, Jimmy, but that's because you haven't earned my *Distrust* yet.

J : You expect me to earn your distrust?

R : If you want to be like *Jumper,* Jimmy. But even *Jumper* needs
some help to earn the *Distrust* of her staff and colleagues.

J : Is that another objective of the *Tergiversator*?

R : You still don't get it, Jimmy. *Jumper's* objective is to earn sufficient
Distrust to create an atmosphere of *Fluctuation* and *Vacillation* and
change the work environment to be perpetually *Disruptive*.

J : Kind of an uncommon objective, but you make it sound so easy.

R : Exactly, Jimmy. When people start referring to *Jumper* as being *Unreliable* and *Unpredictable,* then she knows she is earning their *Distrust*.

J : How unreliable and unpredictable does one need to be to earn distrust?

R : Simple, Jimmy. When *Unreliable* and *Unpredictable* are added to the reference list, then *Jumper* knows she is properly being perceived with *Distrust*.

J : And the way to do that is to be a good at ratting then?

R : Not ratting, Jimmy—*Checking*. Ratting is what stoolpigeon's do.

J : Right. I think my hand is checking out on me

R : Just about done, Jimmy. Only the skit to do.

J : Another Fairy Tale skit? What's this one about?

R : 3Ps.

J : Is that the Peter Principle People again?

R : No, Jimmy, it's 3Ps not P^{3}s. It's a Fairy Tale about the 3 Little Pigs.

J : Oh! Do we have to do another skit? Can't you just describe the scenario?

R : You don't like theater, Jimmy?

J : This is hardly theatre, Red, although it might work
at one of Mark Breslin's Yuk Yuks clubs.

R : That's the right spirit, Jimmy.

J : OK, fine. Let's see it.

R : I'll read it, Jimmy. Once upon a time, a Big Bad Wolf,
whose name is Bobby-Jon, is the manager of—

J : Is Bobby-Jon a *Mizzy*?

R : No, Jimmy. He's a P^3, but many P^{3}s serve as excellent role models for *Mizzies* because the consequences of their behaviour achieves the same type of results that *Mizzies* are looking for.

J :   Is that why it's so difficult to tell P^3s and *Mizzies* apart?

R :   Aye, Jimmy. Now… *Fifer Pig, Fiddler Pig,* and *Practical Pig* are the three little pigs—

J :   Aren't those the names of the little pigs in the Disney movie?

R :   They are, Jimmy. Do you have a problem with that?

J :   No, I don't, but Disney might, as I think Disney owns those names.

R :   OK, Jimmy. We'll just call them all Darryll.

J :   They can't all have the same name.

R :   Why not Jimmy? It worked for Bob Newhart.

J :   Fine, just keep reading.

R :   Now, Jimmy, the set up for the skit is that Bobby-Jon is the Manager of the Sasquatch Sewage Treatment Plant, and he sent out three Requests for Proposals or RFPs for Design-Build Services to renovate and expand the plant's aging infrastructure—

J :   Wait a minute. What's Design-Build?

R :   Good question, Jimmy. Actually I don't think anyone really knows for sure what it is, expect that it doesn't usually work very well on complex projects, so it must be brilliant.

J :   Brilliant for…?

R :   *Mizzies,* Jimmy, it's brilliant for Mizzies.

J :   Ah, but that still doesn't explain what it is.

R :   Well Jimmy, it seems to be a type of contract where the Contractor is both the designer and the construction manager.

J :   You mean like a Contractor who is also the Architect?

R :   No, Jimmy. The contractor hires an Architect to complete the design and then he gets subcontractors to build it, if he successfully wins the bid.

J :   That's interesting. You know, I worked for a construction company for a summer, and I never saw any architects working for the contractor.

R :   Normally they don't, Jimmy. Usually the architects and the engineers work for the owner directly to design the project and then put it out to tender.

J :   I remember being allowed to sit in on a tender closing once, and I know it's a lot of work for the contractor to prepare any bid on a project, even one that has already been designed. So I expect it would be very expensive for the contractor if he also has to pay architects and engineers to design it as well.

R :   I expect you'd be right, Jimmy, except the architects and engineers don't get paid very much anyway.

J :   Why not?

R :   It's a risky business, Jimmy. It's like going to a casino and betting on your chances of getting the work, except the odds are better at the casino.

J :   So what are the odds?

R :   Well Jimmy, if there are ten submissions, the odds are 1 in 10.

J :   That doesn't sound very good

R :   Blackjack has better odds, Jimmy. It's at least 4 in 10, and you don't have to bet tens of thousands of dollars.

J : So in this Design-Build process, is the contract still awarded to the low bidder?

R : I believe it's the cheapest, Jimmy.

J : What about the design?

R : I don't think they really look at the design, Jimmy, just the price.

J : So why complete and submit a design then, if no one really looks at it?

R : I think it's a make work program for architects, Jimmy.

J : But I thought you just said they didn't get paid very much, if anything.

R : Y'see Jimmy. Most architects are *Mizzies*. They're used to doing work and not getting paid properly, unlike doctors, accountants and lawyers, who are always appropriately overpaid.

J : Why do doctors, accountants, and lawyers always make a lot of money then?

R : Their clients know that they aren't doctors, accountants or lawyers, but when people hire an architect, they always think
they know more about architecture than their architect.

J : Maybe they just know what they want.

R : Maybe, Jimmy, but if you know you need a new heart, you don't usually
make doctors submit a fee proposal and then hire the cheapest doctor.

J : That's because their fees are fixed by Alberta Health.

R : True, Jimmy, but once your doctor is selected, you don't
start telling him to remove your heart through your back,
so the scar won't show when you go swimming.

J : Maybe not, but getting back to this process... for this Design-
Build process, the architects and engineers do a whole bunch
of design work for free or almost free, so someone can pick the
cheapest solution without really looking at the design?

R : If it's a publicly funded project, Jimmy, it doesn't really have to be cheap; it just has to look cheap.

J : I suppose the successful design build contractor can recover his
costs if he gets the job, but for the unsuccessful bidders, does the
owner cover any of their costs for preparing a submission?

R : Not usually, Jimmy, unless it's a two stage RFP with a short list for stage
two, but even then it's only a nominal amount for the short listed firms.

J : All those words spoken individually sounded quite familiar, but
when you put in that order they mean nothing to me, so maybe
we should just move on, unless this is really important.

R : You're right, Jimmy, it's not important. So Darryll had a lot of extra
miscellaneous metal in his shop and he won the first contract to replace all the handrails around the secondary and tertiary clarifiers.

J : What are clarifiers?

R : Tanks filled with scum floating on top, Jimmy.

J : Sounds like our old hot tub.

R : Very large tanks, Jimmy, and filled with sludge as I've said.

J : Like hot springs, with room enough to swim?

R : That's just one of the problems, Jimmy.

J : What is?

R : Swimming, Jimmy.

J : Who would swim in sludge? Uh, on second thought, don't answer that.

R : Fine, Jimmy, but that's what started the first dispute.

J : What dispute?

R : Once the contract was awarded, Bobby-Jon told Darryll to redesign the guardrails to comply with code.

J : Didn't the original design meet code then?

R : Depends on who interprets the code, Jimmy. Darryll used the section of the code that governs work places with restricted public access, which are not accessible to children.

J : Makes sense, I guess.

R : Bobby-Jon, on the other hand, decided to apply the code that governs public places like swimming pools, Jimmy.

J : What's the difference?

R : About 100 millimetres, Jimmy.

J : What does that mean, *100 millimetres*?

R : It's the diameter of a ball, Jimmy.

J : What ball? What are you talking about?

R : The maximum size of ball that can go through an opening in a public guardrail is 100 millimetres, Jimmy, but for controlled places it's 200 millimetres.

J : Why would Bobby-Jon want to do this?

R : Do you want the good reason, Jimmy, or the real reason?

J : Neither, but—

R : Tours, Jimmy.

J : Is there a point to this?

R : Well the good reason, Jimmy, is because Bobby-Jon said he wanted to conduct tours for school kids.

J : That's ridiculous. Do I really have to listen to the real reason?

R : He doesn't like Darryll, Jimmy.

J : Which one?

R : All of them, Jimmy.

J : I'm sorry Red, but this skit is just plain stupid, and I don't see any value in putting it in the book.

R : Is it really annoying you then, Jimmy?

J : It really is, Red.

R : Great Jimmy; then we're done with Chapter 25.

J : Really? You're not going to finish the story.

R : No need, Jimmy.

J : Promise?

R : If it's got you frustrated already, Jimmy, then that should be a sufficient *Miz-Experience* for our readers for this chapter.

J :   Good, 'cause I'm done too.

R :   I can't make it on Tuesday, Jimmy—

J :   Sorry, Red, one last question.

R :   I thought we were done Jimmy?

J :   I know, but I'm still curious. What does this story have to do with the three little pigs?

R :   Simple, Jimmy. Darryll was a miscellaneous metal contractor who went bankrupt on the first contract because Bobby-Jon kept making changes and rejecting the work. So he went to work for his brother Darryll, who built pre-fab steel buildings. Darryll got the second contract to design and build the storage buildings, but he also went bankrupt for the same reasons as his brother. So, Darryll and Darryll went to work for their brother Darryll, who was a masonry contractor. He got the third contract to design and build the new brick headworks building—

J :   OK OK, I get the picture. Bobby-Jon got fired and Darryll and his brothers lived happily ever after.

R :   No, Jimmy. Darryll went bankrupt as well.

J :   I'm really sorry I asked.

R :   If y'don't ask, Jimmy, you'll never learn the lessons of real life.

J :   There's nothing real about this, and there isn't even a moral to the story.

R :   Life is not always unfair, Jimmy. But when it is, soak it up. I'll see you at two o'clock on Saturday then? At the Whyte Avenue Second Cup?

J :   Uh…

Technically, Red had just asked two questions, but since he didn't wait for an answer, I accepted them for what they were… rhetorical. Yet another abrupt departure, and Red was gone in a flash. I was absolutely drained and relieved at the same time. I was really ready for a coffee break, but where do you go for a coffee break if you are already at a coffee shop? Good thing there were lots of bars close by.

CHAPTER 51

THE INTIMIDATOR
(THUMPER)

CHEN
THE AROUSING
[SHOCK, THUNDER]

Intimidate

To make timid, frighten, to discourage or inhibit by threats

The week passed quickly, and here we were with another Saturday, another weather report, and more snow. Off I went to the Whyte Avenue Second Cup, with muddled reckonings in my head, a notebook in my hand, and not much consolation in either one. As I approached the entrance, I experienced the same hesitation that I always have, in summertime, just before I am about to jump off a dock into a freezing lake—I try to remember why I want to do this stupid thing and must remind myself that it's my choice to jump or not to jump.

I shivered and opened the door. My first choice would have probably been a root canal, if I had a choice, but unfortunately, Red was already there, sitting next to the window in the far corner, and it was too late; he had already spotted me.

J : Hi Red, I see you found your favourite window spot.

R : It was vacant, Jimmy. Have a seat.

J : You seem to be in need of a coffee, Red.

R : Wonderful idea, Jimmy.

J : I'll get it. Same as usual?

R : That would be grand, Jimmy.

J : Here's your coffee and whatever.

R : You've a big heart, Jimmy.

J : And a smaller wallet. So today is intimidation day is it?

R : Aye, Jimmy, but it seems to be a behaviour that's more prevalent in the *Brillie* world than in the *Mizzie* world, and it's probably the hardest behavioural trait for a *Mizzie* to master.

J : Why is that?

R : Hard to say for sure, Jimmy, but I suppose it's because *Mizzies* are more focused on making their own lives miserable than on making others miserable. They often don't appreciate the *Miz-Benefits* of forcefully instilling *Mizery* in the lives of those around them.

J : Through intimidation?

R : Aye, Jimmy. Intimidation is a technique that breeds contempt, which contributes significantly to building an effective *Miz-Environment*.

J : Makes sense I suppose, in a Red Knech kind of way.

R : Absolutely, Jimmy, but since most *Mizzies* seem reluctant to adopt this behaviour, we have to get them to B-A-T.

J : Are we shifting from hockey to baseball now or do you mean "*go-to-bat*," for someone?

R : Don't be daft, Jimmy. I said B-A-T.

J : Which spells bat, right?

R : Brilliant, Jimmy. You can spell rat and now you can spell bat.

J : Uh oh, is this a behavioural practice?

R : You really are a bit slow today, Jimmy. It is and I'm talking about *Bullying, Annoying* and *Tormenting*.

J : The behavioural practices of the *Intimidator*, right?

R : That was hardly a challenge, Jimmy.

J : The coffee's just starting to kick in. OK. So let's go to BAT.

R : Right then, Jimmy. As I was about to say, most *Mizzies* seem to shy away from *Bullying, Annoying* and *Tormenting*, as those practices are more in line with the behaviour of a sadist, not a masochist.

J : Have we established that B-A-T stands for *Bullying, Annoying* and *Tormenting*?

R : Didn't I just say that, Jimmy?

J : Uh, I suppose you did! Is repeating what you say annoying?

R : I think you're catching on, Jimmy. Although *Mizzies* often establish relationships with sadistic types, who are usually quite effective at enhancing *Mizery*, they don't easily associate themselves with sadistic behaviours.

J : So how can *Mizzies* learn to adopt these unfamiliar practices?

R : Subtle intimidation, Jimmy.

J : Sounds like an oxymoron.

R : No doubt you're an expert on morons, Jimmy, but subtle and intimidation are not actually contradictory terms. In fact they can be quite complimentary under the right circumstances.

J : Of course, and the right circumstances would be...?

R : The workplace, Jimmy. You don't seem to be taking it all in, and you have to pay attention then.

J : Sorry, Red.

R : Not to worry, Jimmy. Just read through your notes a few times until it sinks in.

J : Right then, moving on.

R : Y'see Jimmy, while most real bullies desperately want everyone to know that they really are bullies, *Mizzies* just want to realize the same *Miz-Impact* on the work environment that occurs as a result of *Bullying*.

J : So they need to *Bully* their staff, without really behaving like a *Bully*.

R : Brilliant, Jimmy. Y'really can listen when you want to.

J : Sounds a bit like the Irish art of persuasion.

R : It is exactly like that, Jimmy. When a masterful *Mizzy* uses subtle *Bullying* techniques in an effective manner, their staff will say thank you and even ask for more.

J : Intriguing! So, how does that work?

R : Quite effectively, Jimmy. It's not the blatant and obvious approach of the brash *Bully*.

J : OK. Once again we now know what it's not, but what is it?

R : Y'see Jimmy, you don't actually have to physically beat a person up to be a *Bully*; you just have to make them feel like they've been beaten up.

J : Sounds good, Red, but I think it might help our readers if they had an example of how to do this effectively.

R : E-mail, Jimmy.

J : You're going to E-mail an example to me?

R : No, Jimmy. E-mail is an example.

J : E-mail is an example?

R : Y'don't have to repeat everything I say just

to prove you're listening, Jimmy.

J :   Really? OK, thanks.

R :   Brilliant, Jimmy.

J :   What's brilliant?

R :   You're response, Jimmy?

J :   'OK' is brilliant?

R :   No no, Jimmy... "Thanks."

J :   Thanks for what?

R :   Coffee still not kicking in, Jimmy? I suppose it was unintentional that you thanked me for criticizing you then.

J :   That was supposed to be a sarcastic thank you.

R :   With just a hint of bitterness, Jimmy. This, by the way, is exactly the type of reaction that enhances a *Miz-Environment*. A sarcastic or derisive offer of pretentious gratitude in response to a disparaging remark or malicious e-mail is an indication that the technique of subtle *Bullying* has been successfully applied.

J :   Really? Who knew?

R :   No one, Jimmy. That's why *Mizzies* need this book.

J :   Of course. Now you mentioned e-mail as an example, but I was wondering if it would be helpful to our readers if they understand why e-mail is subtle?

R :   Not yet, Jimmy.

J :   Why not?

R :   If you give *Miz-Readers* everything in logical order, how does that contribute to their *Miz-Experience* when they read the book?

J :   Well that may be good for *Mizzies*, but since I'm not a *Mizzy*, I would appreciate it if you would indulge me.

R :   Right, Jimmy. If you don't understand something, just say so and don't pretend it's the readers who need to know.

J :   Guilty as charged. So why is e-mail so subtle?

R :   Y'see Jimmy, most bullies prefer to confront their victims directly because they enjoy watching the squirming reactions of their victims.

J :   Sounds a bit sadistic all right.

R :   Definitely, Jimmy. But *Mizzies*, on the other hand, find that watching someone suffer only makes them jealous, unless they too can share in the in *Mizery*.

J :   Subtle.

R :   It's even more subtle, Jimmy if *Miz-Managers* don't actually speak to their intended victims and if they can arrange to be unavailable when the e-mail is opened. This is especially effective and much safer, since the recipient has no avenue to vent their frustration, and they can't inflict any physical damage on the *Miz-Manager*.

J :   You mean send it from your blackberry?

R :   Brilliant, Jimmy. Also, when using e-mail, *Miz-Managers* can be even more hurtful and nit-picky, as they can take the time to carefully craft the wording to have the most impact. A further added benefit is that the recipient will likely read it more than a few times and each time they read it, they will become increasingly more *Annoyed* and upset.

J : Like twisting the knife, after you stab someone.

R : Good analogy, Jimmy.

J : Now I can see how this might be effective on an individual basis, but having to pick on your victims one-at-a-time, seems like a lot of work.

R : Good point, Jimmy. So a good *Miz-Manager* may occasionally leave behind a draft copy of the e-mail by the printer or accidentally copy the office busy-body and then make a feeble attempt to recall the e-mail.

J : Recall seldom seems to work anyway.

R : Precisely, Jimmy, which means it will spread quickly through the rumour mill.

J : Does this technique work on groups as well as individuals.

R : Not really, Jimmy. Bullies only pick on the weak and vulnerable, and it's not as effective if you try to pick on a group of people, unless they are all very weak.

J : So *Bullying* is more of a one-on-one technique then?

R : It has to be personal, Jimmy. But when a *Bully* picks on one or two vulnerable victims, it's important to make sure that everyone knows about it, because they will also get upset and become miserable in support of the victims.

J : So it does work on groups, if you spread the misery around eh?

R : Exactly, Jimmy. We know that *Mizery* is contagious, and by *Bullying, Annoying* and *Tormenting* just one or two victims, and inflicting a small amount of initial *Mizery*, it can multiply exponentially with amazing *Miz-Effectiveness*.

J : OK. E-mail sounds like it really works, are there some other examples?

R : Indeed, Jimmy. Voice mail is also effective, but you must be sure the victims are away from their desks. It can be especially *Annoying* if you speak slowly, but inarticulately so that when the message time runs out, you have to phone back to complete your tirade in a second message.

J : I can see how that would be very annoying.

R : Leaving terse, unsigned notes at their desk, Jimmy, with derogatory comments or demanding orders can also do the trick.

J : If the note isn't signed, how will they know who placed it there?

R : It doesn't really matter, Jimmy. And if somehow it should find its way into the wrong hands, the *Miz-Manager* is protected by plausible deniability.

J : So is that it for *Bullying*?

R : No, Jimmy, but we have to let *Miz-Managers* work on coming up with some of their own creative methods for subtle *Bullying* or there will be no *Miz-Effort* required on their part.

J : Right, so what about *Annoying* and *Tormenting*?

R : Well Jimmy, *Annoying* is quite well understood by *Brillies*, as they are accustom to assuming that whatever is *An-*

noying to themselves is equally *Annoying* to others.

J : Kind of like the Golden Rule in reverse?

R : Spot-on again, Jimmy, but it's not that easy for *Mizzies*. The problem is that things that annoy *Brillies* are not *Annoying* to *Mizzies,* since they relish in annoyance.

J : So you're saying that because Mizzies don't understand what really annoys Brillies, they can't be as annoying as they would like to be?

R : Actually they can, Jimmy. They are, in fact, constantly *Annoying* to Brillies. The problem is that they just don't know it. Once they are made aware that the behaviour of *Mizzies* is almost always annoying to *Brillies,* they don't have to worry about it.

J : Well, they know now, because you just told them

R : Only if they read the book Jimmy.

J : Fair enough. So how do they learn what techniques work most effectively?

R : No need, Jimmy. All they have to know is that whatever behaviour comes naturally to them will be effective, so just do it more often.

J : Easy enough. Kind of like our discussions, eh?

R : Is it working, Jimmy?

J : Quite effectively. What about *Tormenting* then?

R : Equally easy, Jimmy, if a *Miz-Manager* has grown up with siblings. Older siblings have a natural, inherent ability for *Tormenting* their younger siblings. Simply recalling childhood memories can trigger an unlimited source of ways and means to torment subordinates.

J : What if a *Miz-Manager* was an only child?

R : Good question, Jimmy. In that case, they can draw on examples from friends or cousins who were tormented by their elder siblings.

J : What if they were orphans?

R : You're pushing it, Jimmy.

J : Does that mean I'm annoying?

R : Brilliant, Jimmy, but not to me, of course. I think you get the drift though.

J : Great, how about if we drift over to the counter for a refill.

R : Excellent idea, Jimmy, but that's not *Annoying*.

J : Maybe not to you, Red, but I'm sure it will be for the young lady behind the counter.

R : Not if I went by myself, Jimmy.

J : Are you offering to go?

R : No, Jimmy. We wouldn't want to deprive the young lady of the pleasure of your company.

J : Coffee's here, Red.

R : Ta, Jimmy. No muffins?

J : Patience, Red, I only have two hands.

R : Thanks, Jimmy.

J : Moving along then, does the *Intimidator* have a nemesis?

R : One with an attitude of *Sedulous Altruism,* Jimmy.

J : Ah ha! You probably think I don't know what that means?

R : Why would I think that, Jimmy? I'm sure that
both words are in your wee dictionary.

J : No doubt they are, but I already know what
they mean without looking them up.

R : We could change it to *Virtuous Fanaticism* if y'like, Jimmy.

J : But they don't mean the same thing.

R : Doesn't matter, Jimmy.

J : Why not?

R : We can't change it anyway.

J : How come?

R : Because, Jimmy, that's the nemesis for the *Prevaricator* in chapter 21. How about *Meticulous Perfectionism*?

J : That's not the same either.

R : Close enough, Jimmy.

J : Why does each character need a double word nemesis anyway? So far, the attitude for each nemesis you've described
could be a nemesis for any of these characters.

R : Brilliant, Jimmy.

J : Am I wrong?

R : Not at all, Jimmy, they are quite interchangeable.

J : So why pick Sedulous Altruism for the Intimidator?

R : You're missing the point, Jimmy.

J : Which is?

R : The point is, Jimmy, that any highly energized keen-
ers are usually immune to *Thumper's* behaviour, so it
would be best not to waste much time on them.

J : Is Thumper a rabbit or is this another common name?

R : Good, Jimmy. You remembered.

J : So if Thumper's behaviour is not effective against an attitude of Sedulous Altruism, why mention it?

R : You need to know who your opponents are.

J : So Thumper needs to know who these people are that he
can't do anything about, so he can do what exactly?

R : Focus on the weak, Jimmy.

J : Like the cowardly lion?

R : That's it, Jimmy.

J : But how do *Miz-Managers* offset the impact of
one who practices *Sedulous Altruism*?

R : Fortunately, Jimmy, *Slashing* has a contagious effect on everyone who sympathizes with the victims.

J : Slashing sounds suspiciously like another hockey penalty?

R : Good guess, Jimmy. *Slashing* is the code name that *Thumper* uses for *Bullying, Annoying* and *Tormenting*.

J : That makes sense, since hitting an opponent with a stick
is akin to the cowardly act of an intimidating *Bully*.

R : It is indeed, Jimmy.

J : Does sympathy for victims work on those with
an attitude of *Sedulous Altruism*?

R : Especially them, Jimmy, as they are always very sympa-
thetic, and when they try to go to bat for the weak, they just
need to be reminded that it's none of their business.

J : Right then, did we BAT this around enough for today?

R : Not quite, Jimmy.

J : Why is that, Red?

R : I'm not finished my coffee, Jimmy.

J : So what should we discuss then?

R : Perception, Jimmy.

J : Meaning?

R : If the *Intimidator* wants to earn the *Detestation* of her staff, she
must modify her behaviour to be *Hostile* and *Callous*.

J : That could be a tall order to fill.

R : True for some, Jimmy. But there are quite a lot of folks
around who are just naturally detestable.

J : I think I know a few.

R : Makes it easier for you, Jimmy.

J : Why's that?

R : You have someone to model your behaviour after then, Jimmy.

J : Lucky me.

R : Lucky indeed, Jimmy, but unfortunately many
Mizzies don't have that advantage.

J : Perhaps I could introduce you to them.

R : That won't help unless they practice, Jimmy?

J : Practice what?

R : *Batting*, Jimmy.

J : OK, hold it, Red. In the last chapter you wouldn't let me
use ratting, but now it's OK for you to use batting?

R : It is, Jimmy.

J : Why?

R : Because, Jimmy, batting is what *Intimidators* do,
but ratting is not what *Tergiversators* do.

J : Red Knech logic then?

R : *Miz-Logic*, Jimmy, but you can use *Slashing* if you prefer.

J : Thanks a lot.

R : Contemptuous Sarcasm works too, Jimmy.

J : That's a bit harsh, Red, I was just kidding around.

R : Not you, Jimmy. That's *Thumper's* attitude, although I must say, you're progressing.

J : OK, sorry, if attitude fuels actions, what are Thumper's actions then?

R : To Frighten, Annoy and Abuse, Jimmy.

J : I imagine that Thumper could score a lot of goals with that type of behaviour, and it would definitely be disruptive.

R :   It might, but those aren't the goals, Jimmy.

J :   What are they?

R :   Think about it, Jimmy. You *Frighten* someone so they will be what?

J :   Afraid?

R :   Good, Jimmy. What else?

J :   Is this a test?

R :   No, Jimmy. I'm just trying to create a challenge for
you so you can appreciate a little *Mizery* here.

J :   I have no shortage of misery, but it's not quite the same as being scared, fearful, victimized or persecuted is it?

R :   One contributes to the other, but you really seem to understand the fear factor. Can you do *Annoy* and *Abuse* as well?

J :   Let's see. When someone annoys me I feel annoyed, provoked, incensed, distressed—

R :   Quick response, Jimmy. Is this a common feeling for you?

J :   It seems to be lately, but I don't seem to be
abused as often as I get annoyed.

R :   We'll have to work on that then, Jimmy. Usually if someone is
abused, they feel *Mistreated, Harmed, Injured* and *Hurt.*

J :   Well, come to think of it, I have experienced a bit of that recently. Are those the offence goals or the defence goals?

R :   Offence, Jimmy. *Belligerent* and *Confrontational* are the defence goals.

J :   And how one does reach those heights?

R :   Thumper must learn to *Extort* and *Browbeat* effectively.

J :   Excellent. Where can I sign up for lessons?

R :   Just finish the book, Jimmy.

J :   Well let's move on then. Can we go over *Thumper's* objectives?

R :   Absolutely, Jimmy. She's looking to create an atmosphere of *Oppression* and *Domination.*

J :   Something to look forward to for sure. I can imagine that
the Miz-Environment is even more delightful.

R :   Subjugation, Jimmy.

J :   Sounds like another amazing, but obscure, management objective.

R :   That's why we're writing this book, Jimmy.

J :   Right, do you really think slashing will be enough to do the trick
to create this atmosphere of *Oppression* and *Domination?*

R :   Should be, Jimmy, if it's done right.

J :   So with just a little batting practice, Thumper can
use slashing to become an *Intimidator,* right?

R :   It'll take a bit more than *Slashing,* Jimmy, for her to become a really effective Intimidator.

J :   Do you believe that women make better Intimidators than men?'

R :   They make the best subtle *Intimidators,* Jimmy.

J :   OK. Does that help her to earn her *Detestation* stripes?

R : If she can master the art of being *Hostile* and *Callous.*

J : Sounds really inspirational.

R : Indeed, Jimmy. Just think of how many famous *In-timidators* are still inspirational today.

J : Such as?

R : Caesar, Jimmy—

J : I hate to break it to you, Red, but Caesar was not a woman.

R : Neither were Genghis Khan, Napoleon, Hitler, or Osama Bin Laden, Jimmy, but they were also not very subtle.

J : Whoa there, Red, now you're really pushing it. Maybe they are inspirational to a small number of fanatical nuts, but it's really inappropriate to include them in a book about man-agement behaviour. Especially in a family book.

R : Perhaps, Jimmy. But, we're not advocating extremism.

J : Technically it's still a Miz-mm, is it not?

R : Not for this book, Jimmy. The point is not to underestimate the power of those who aspire to *Lead* and be *Inspirational.*

J : Whose objective is that?

R : Not objectives, Jimmy; those are the *goals* of our nemesis.

J : The ones that we are batting and slashing?

R : No, Jimmy, we're *Slashing* the weak, which upsets the *Intimidator's* nemesis, because their behaviour is always *Affable* and *Considerate.*

J : What do they want?

R : An atmosphere of *Illumination* and *Communication,* Jim-my, thriving in an *Invigorative* environment.

J : I'm going out on a limb here, but I'm guessing we don't want that, do we?

R : Absolutely not, Jimmy, there's too high a risk that *Leader-ship* and *Inspiration* will undo all of *Thumper's Miz-Efforts.*

J : We sure can't have an epidemic of that sort, can we?

R : No, Jimmy.

J : What else then?

R : Synonyms, Jimmy.

J : Synonyms for what?

R : For the behaviours of an *Intimidator,* Jimmy.

J : Is this a test?

R : Just an exercise, Jimmy.

J : OK. I'll play along. Let's see, there's tyrannizing… torturing… uh… harassing… frightening… threatening… How am I doing?

R : Just about done, Jimmy.

J : How many do you want?

R : That's good, Jimmy.

J : What do you want me to do with them?

R : Nothing, Jimmy, I was just keeping you busy until I finished my coffee.

J : Now that's really annoying.

R : And effective, Jimmy. Just like the mad hatter.

J : Oh no, not another one of your stupid fairy-tales.

R : Alice's Adventure in Wonderland, Jimmy.

J : Do we really have to do a skit? Everyone knows that the Queen of Hearts was a bully.

R : Quite true, Jimmy. But that's only what we know from Alice's short time there, as described by Charles Dodgson.

J : Who's he?

R : Lewis Carroll, Jimmy.

J : Why did you say Charles whatever?

R : That's his real name, Jimmy; Charles Dodgson.

J : So what do you know that the rest of us don't?

R : Well Jimmy, you probably know that it is considered to be one of the best examples of the literary nonsense genre.

J : Something that I'm sure you know a lot about as well, Red.

R : True, Jimmy. But Charles couldn't include everything there is to know about Wonderland in one short book.

J : So what's missing?

R : We don't know for sure, Jimmy, but we can speculate.

J : You mean *guess*, or even assume?

R : Why not, Jimmy?

J : Because you told me not to, remember?

R : True, Jimmy, but that was different.

J : In what way?

R : They were *your* assumptions, Jimmy.

J : Thanks for nothing.

R : We use logic, Jimmy, to determine the techniques that an intimidator like the Queen of Hearts would most likely apply if she were here in the real world.

J : Like what?

R : For example, Jimmy, assume she is a government leader and that some people are opposing her position on certain issues.

J : What issues?

R : You pick them, Jimmy. Pick three.

J : OK. Health Care… uh… Education and… Environment.

R : Good ones, Jimmy. The first thing she would probably do is eliminate all the potentially controversial words from their dictionary and thus from their language.

J : What kind of words?

R : Words and phrases like Dictator, Jimmy… and Challenge, Complaint, Bully, Global Warming, Crowded Classrooms, Wait Times, Full Coverage and—

J : Nasty words all right.

R : But worst of all, Jimmy, the word *Quality*, when used in association with controversial issues.

J : You mean like Quality Education, Quality Environment and Quality Health Care?

R : Exactly, Jimmy.

J : Certainly can't have people using those words in Wonderland.

R : No she can't, Jimmy.

J : Good. Now what does she do?

R : Changes the language, Jimmy, using social media and texting?

J : How can that change language?

R : U shud tx mor Jimy.

J : Fair enough. What's next?

R : We'll start with Health Care, Jimmy. If Doctors are using nasty words about the health care system, she might have new types of high tech surgical masks developed for their use.

J : How does that help?

R : They'd be required to wear them at all times, Jimmy, not just during surgery.

J : Many Doctors aren't surgeons and never need to wear masks.

R : Times are changing, Jimmy, and these are masks made from special high tech materials.

J : What kind of special materials?

R : Green duct tape, Jimmy.

J : That's just plain ridiculous.

R : Nonsense genre, Jimmy. It's symbolism.

J : Is that another Miz-mm?

R : Speak no evil, Jimmy.

J : Fine, don't tell me. So what about education?

R : iPods, Jimmy.

J : iPods? How can iPods control controversy?

R : Subliminal intervention, Jimmy.

J : Is that like subliminal advertising?

R : Very similar, Jimmy. She just makes sure that all the iPods are pre-programmed with subliminal messages before they are issued, and that confuses educators so they only hear what they need to know.

J : Hear no evil?

R : Not really, Jimmy. They all hear *different* evil, so they can never agree on anything.

J : Divided they fall, is that it?

R : It is, Jimmy.

J : What about number three, the Environment?

R : Laser surgery, Jimmy.

J : How does that work?

R : Quite effectively, Jimmy. It's like having permanent rose-coloured sunglasses or contact lenses, except that they're green. Whatever an environmentalist sees looks greener, which makes them feel better, thus reducing their desire to complain about the lack of support for greening the environment.

J :   Sounds simple if all environmentalists agree to laser surgery.

R :   It'll be free and mandatory, Jimmy.

J :   What if they already have 20/20 vision?

R :   Have you ever seen an environmentalist who didn't wear glasses, Jimmy?

J :   Well uh… OK, but you know this will never work, don't you?

R :   Of course I know that, Jimmy. The point is that *Thumper* can't just cut people's heads off like the Queen of Hearts. She needs to come up with some creative concepts to intimidate and impose control.

J :   However, you just suggested three very uh… very creative, but pretty much useless ideas. How does that help?

R :   It's like an allegory, Jimmy, with each key word being a symbol of the objective.

J :   Sounds deep, Red. Like deep dish cow pie.

R :   Exactly, Jimmy. Y'see how you just used the word *'cow pie,'* but we both know that's not what you really wanted to say. It's the polite symbol for words that start with B and S, right?

J :   OK, fair enough. What are your key words symbols of?

R :   The green duct tape Jimmy, signifies muzzling, but there are many ways to muzzle people.

J :   For example?

R :   Just threaten the doctors, Jimmy. Tell them that they will lose their jobs or be transferred to some remote location.

J :   That's not very subtle.

R :   If you want subtle, Jimmy, try encryption.

J :   Encryption of what?

R :   E-mail, Jimmy. If you want to keep your education foes in check, just encrypt all your e-mails so nobody has access to all the same information, which has the added bonus of inducing paranoia. This may also work for the Environmentalists.

J :   Well I'm none of those, and it works on me.

R :   Good, Jimmy. I'll see you on Tuesday next at 2 o'clock. Telus Plaza?

As usual, he didn't wait for an answer before he scurried toward the escalator and vanished quickly from sight. Although I was no longer surprised by Red's hasty departures after each of our sessions, it was still a bit disconcerting, and it left me with a bit of an unexplainable deserted feeling. My only consolation was one scrappy folded note, accidentally left behind by Red. It sat there on the table, staring at me and daring me to open it. I glanced down at it every few minutes, but it seemed like an hour before I unfolded it and began to read Red's scrawled out incomplete dissertation.

'Once upon a time, in the land of Hart, there was a beloved Queen. The Queendom of Hart was an idyllic paradise where words and phrases like **Dictator, Challenge, Complaint, Bully, Wait Times, Full Coverage,** *and—worst of all—***Quality Patient Care** *were never used because they did not exist in the Hart language. The Queen must have had some psychic powers because she seemed to know exactly what the people needed without ever*

even listening to them. Following one of her psychic visions, she conceded to the will of her people to edit and remove all such nasty words and phrases from the Hart dictionary.

One day, after receiving yet another of her psychic visions, she decided to create a National Health Care System to show how much she loved and cared for her people. The Queen always held within her heart the best interests of her people. She spoke for the people of Hart from her heart and when they lost their way, she gave them hers. The polls told her that her popularity with her people was exceeded only by the beloved rulers in the distant lands of Syria, Libya, Egypt and North Korea.

The Queen stayed closely in touch with her people by flying all around the Queendom of Hart in one of her many jets. She would spend hours listening to the silence of her people not using all those nasty words and phrases that were not in the dictionary.

Then one day, while the Queen was on a short six month trade mission to the land of Margaritas, she received a disturbing message from one of her white robots about some rogue doctors using some nasty words at the end of their 48 hour shifts. The results of a public inquisition concluded that the doctors' surgical masks were impeding their ability to communicate accurately, so the loving Queen ordered new masks for her doctors. The new masks, to be worn at all times, were made of beautiful state-of-the-art green duct tape.

Harmony returned to the Queendom of Hart, and the Queen was heard to say, as she boarded her jet, 'Ah… my lovely doctors—I can't live without them, and I can't work them to death.'

The end

Chapter 3

The Repudiator
(Bumper)

Chun
[Difficulty at the Beginning]

Repudiate

To refuse to have anything to do with, to reject the validity of, to disown, to reject, to cast off

Consistent with Edmonton's sometimes barbarous winter climate, it was cold and snowing on Tuesday. Fortunately, the Light Rail Transit connects directly to Telus Plaza, so like the moles that we Canadians often are in winter, I skillfully navigated the underground caverns until I arrived at the Second Cup on the lower level of Telus Plaza for yet another unpredictable session with the pervasive Mr. Red Knech.

I think Red likes the Second Cup at Telus Plaza, because Daryl, one of the owners, once gave him a free latte and he always remembers to call him by his name. It's better for me too because Daryl knows exactly what Red likes, so I don't have to refer to my notes. Now that I'm finally learning to speak a little bit of Second Cup, I hope Red doesn't change his preference and move our sessions to Starbucks, 'cause I must admit that I'm still struggling with their terminology.

As I emerged from the underground urban maze and caught a glimpse of the proverbial light at the end of the tunnel, the light quickly dimmed as a familiar figure came into focus, sitting at a table outside Second Cup next to the window.

J : Afternoon, Red. It's really snowing out there.

R : I don't need a weather report, Jimmy. I can see through the window, but I'm glad to see y'too.

J : I see you already have your coffee and muffin.

R : Aye, Jimmy. Daryl said you could square it with him whenever you're ready for your own coffee.

J : Good old, Daryl.

R : Indeed, Jimmy. He upgraded it to a large, so you only have to pay for a medium... and the muffin of course.

J : What a deal. I'll be right back.

R : No rush, Jimmy.

J : So Red, we are on to the *Repudiator*, is that right?

R : *Bumper,* Jimmy.

J : You call him... or her, *Bumper*?

R : It's her common name, Jimmy.

J : Right, for the *Repudiator*?

R : It's a synonym, Jimmy, for refute or reject.

J : Great, more synonyms. I should have bought you a synonym bun. Do I have to come up with more synonyms until you finish your coffee again?

R : I just started my coffee, Jimmy. I don't think there are enough synonyms to keep you busy that long.

J : There's a relief. Tell me, Red, do you always behave like this, or is this side of you demeanour reserved especially for me?

R : That's Antagonistic and Thoughtless, Jimmy.

J : I don't think it's anymore antagonistic or thoughtless than you making me list a bunch of synonyms for—

R : What are you on about now, Jimmy? Those are the behaviours of the *Repudiator*.

J : Antagonistic and Thoughtless?

R : What did I just say, Jimmy?

J : Got it. Great reference for someone who wants a career in public relations.

R : Exactly, Jimmy. Do you always get distracted so easily, or was it just that cute wee Lass with the short skirt over there?

J : Short skirts are my weakness.

R : You really thought I was calling you *Antagonistic* and *Thoughtless,* Jimmy?

J : Well I—

R : I'm sorry; I didn't think you were that sensitive. I hope I didn't hurt your feeling.

J : My feeling?

R : Do you have more than just the one then, Jimmy?

J : Can we move along here?

R : You're a wee bit red again, Jimmy.

J : Ouch! What was that for?

R : That was just my elbow, Jimmy.

J : But that really hurt.

R : What do I get for it?

J : Oh cute, more penalties. Two minutes for elbowing, is that it?

R : Brilliant yet again, Jimmy.

J : Strange way to make your point.

R : And what is *Elbowing,* Jimmy?

J : Using an elbow in any way to foul an opponent. So am I your opponent now?

R : It's just ramming practice, Jimmy. Don't take it so seriously.

J : Ramming?

R : Reproaching, Admonishing, and Maligning, Jimmy. R-A-M.

J : Behavioural Practices?

R : Exactly, Jimmy.

J : You know, Red, I don't mind the verbal insults and whatever, but I'm not really into body contact sports.

R : Sorry, Jimmy. I thought you were a fan. Let's shift to *Insulting, Berating,* and *Defaming.*

J : Can we please get back to the Repudiator?

R : What do y'think I'm doing then, Jimmy?

J : Oh, so insulting, berating, and defaming are what?

R : Actions, Jimmy. That's how *Bumper* achieves her goals and makes people feel like you're feeling now.

J : Insulted?

R : That, Jimmy, and Offended, Harassed, Affronted, and Disrespected.

J : How about berated?

R : Not yet, Jimmy. We're not finished with insulting.

J : I have a suspicion that we'll never be finished with insults.

R : We're done with the little ones, Jimmy.

J : What's a big one?

R : Uniforms are good ones, Jimmy.

J : Map please?

R : Lost are you, Jimmy?

J : Are you pretending to be surprised?

R : Not really, Jimmy. Getting back to uniforms, a great example of a big insult was when the White Star Line asked the parents of one of their musicians who died on the Titanic to pay for his lost uniform.

J : Are you kidding me?

R : Y'should know by now that I never kid, Jimmy.

J : Did that get out to the press?

R : Of course, Jimmy. That's how the Brits learned to use this technique.

J : Whoa! You mean someone else did something similar.

R : No, Jimmy. Not similar—*exactly the same*—and just recently too.

J : Really?

R : During the war in the Falkland Islands, a young British soldier was killed and the army, having learned from White Star, billed his family for the cost of the uniform that was destroyed.

J : That is really, really insulting, but I don't see how Bumper can do anything like that in the workplace today.

R : You'd be surprised, Jimmy. On a smaller scale, if you were re-organizing the partnership in a small company and one of the potential partners was not cooperating—

J : What do you mean by *'not cooperating?'*

R : Someone who is holding out for a fair and reasonable deal, Jimmy.

J : Sounds very naive. Then what?

R : Complete the company name change, without adding the obstinate holdout's name and then publish an announcement in the paper without advising the obnoxious holdout.

J : You mean our holdout finds out by reading it first in the paper?

R : Exactly, Jimmy.

J : Wow, and that's your idea of a smaller scale insult?

R : There's always caustic comments, Jimmy, for the wee insults, but you've already mastered them.

J : I'm certainly not in your league, Red.

R : That's very kind of you, Jimmy.

J : Do you have some examples?

R : Reviewing a report provides a great opportunity, Jimmy. If you are reviewing a short 12-page report prepared by one of your employees, and he asks what you think, simply reply that you are up to page 21.

J : But you just said it was only 12 pages.

R : That's just what the employee would say as well, Jimmy. To which you reply, *'page 21 of my comments.'*

J : Good one.

R : Or y'could just ask for a copy of the English version, Jimmy.

J : That happens a lot in Canada.

R : Not in Alberta, Jimmy.

J : Dare I even ask about Berate?

R :   Only if you want to feel *Rebuked,* Jimmy. Or perhaps *Criticized, Reproached,* or *Admonished.*

J :   Another 'feeling good moment' brought to you by Red
Knech, but I think you missed defaming me.

R :   Don't rush me, Jimmy, but if I had done, you'd also feel *Ma-
ligned, Denigrated, Disparaged* and *Badmouthed.*

J :   Thanks, Red. I'm feeling better already.

R :   That's the spirit, Jimmy. Let's go for more goals.

J :   Let's just do that.

R :   Keep it up and you'll soon adopt *Bumper's* attitude of *Spurious Scepticism.*

J :   Not likely.

R :   There's still time, Jimmy.

J :   I'll bet that we haven't even looked at the defence goals yet.

R :   That's a winning bet, Jimmy.

J :   And?

R :   Well Jimmy, the options are to either *Ignore* or *Slander.*

J :   Haven't you already done both?

R :   Not to you, Jimmy. It's a choice that *Bumper* has to
make, but you are right, she could do both.

J :   Regardless of which one she chooses, or even if she
uses both, what does she hope to achieve?

R :   Her goals, Jimmy. To either *Dismiss* our *Brillie* friends or *Vilify* them.

J :   Good plan. Hope it works.

R :   She'll soon know if she earns their *Denigration.*

J :   Deservedly earned, no doubt.

R :   The proof is in the pudding, Jimmy.

J :   What kind of pudding are we talking about?

R :   An atmosphere pudding, Jimmy, flavoured with *Rejection* and *Refutation.*

J :   How is it served?

R :   On a *Depressive* platter, Jimmy. I think you're really getting into this.

J :   Scary, isn't it?

R :   Not really, Jimmy, unless our *Brillie* friends throw a mon-
key wrench into the works to scuttle our progress.

J :   What underhanded schemes are they plotting then?

R :   Well first of all, Jimmy, they bring with them their nau-
seating attitude of *Ingenuous Eudemonism.*

J :   Makes me retch just thinking about it.

R :   It does, doesn't it, Jimmy?

J :   Then what?

R :   They want to improve *Productivity* and try to convince everyone to share *Responsibilities.*

J :   At school, we used to call these kids suckho—

R :   Uh uh Jimmy. *Party poopers* would be more appropriate.

J :   Right, I know, it's a family book, and you want me
to be a good Brillie and behave responsibly.

R : It's not what I want, Jimmy; it's what needs to be done
to exemplify the type of outrageous behaviour that op-
poses *Bumper's* efforts on a regular basis.

J : That's a most formidable opponent all right. I'd be absolutely hor-
rified to find some ingenuously eudemonistic smart-ass increas-
ing production and behaving responsibly behind my back.

R : Indeed you would, Jimmy, but it gets even worse.

J : Is that possible?

R : Not only are they productive and responsible, but they run around
behaving in a most unnaturally *Congenial* and *Compassionate* manner.

J : Could it possibly get any worse?

R : It could, Jimmy, indeed. If nothing is done to stop this invasion of
perverted behaviour, Bumper may soon find herself engulfed in an
atmosphere of *Integration* and *Collaboration,* and before she knows it,
she's trapped in an intolerably cheerful and *Responsive* environment.

J : It's unfathomable.

R : Fortunately, Jimmy, it's a rare occurrence and
it is almost always short lived.

J : That's a relief. So what children's story would be inspirational for Bumper?

R : The Ugly Duckling, Jimmy.

J : Really?

R : Y'see Jimmy, most people tell this story incorrectly. Some *Brillie* do-
gooder went and rewrote the ending to change the duckling into a swan.

J : So the ugly duckling wasn't really a swan?

R : No Jimmy. It really was an ugly duckling, repudiated by all the
other ducks, just like Rudolf. Unfortunately for the ugly duckling, it did not have a red nose or any other redeeming qualities and was not only repudiated by the other ducks but by
the hunter who shot it and threw it away in disgust.

J : Hey, wait a minute, Red! That's pushing it way outside the line. Who's going to believe your version?

R : Have you ever even seen a cygnet, Jimmy?

J : A what?

R : Get your wee dictionary out, Jimmy. It's a young swan.

J : Really?

R : Aye really, Jimmy, and they are all cute as a button. No
one would ever call a cygnet ugly, so it couldn't have
been anything but a genuinely ugly duckling.

J : OK, fine. Is that it for the Repudiator?

R : It is Jimmy. We'll do *Damper* on Saturday then. 2 o'clock at Whyte Avenue.

J : Fine…

Off he went once again, like a phantom in the night, except that it was still afternoon.
I knew enough not to try to respond to him with more than one monosyllabic word,
because he was always out of earshot before a second syllable could escape my lips.

As I sat there in blessed silence, I couldn't shake the image of that poor little ugly duckling, who would never become a swan. I desperately needed a drink.

CHAPTER 27

THE DEMORALIZER (DAMPER)

I
THE CORNERS OF THE MOUTH [PROVIDING NOURISHMENT]

Demoralize

To debase the morals of; corrupt, to undermine the confidence of; dishearten, to put into disorder; confuse

With exams coming up, I had been up late every night studying, and I was actually ready for a break, although I'm not sure that a session with Red Knech can really be called a break. I go up late and left late, so I can't imagine what made me think I would be on time for my session with Red. Of course I was late, but only 10 minutes.

Even before I entered the Second Cup, I spotted Red sitting in his favourite corner seat by the window reading the Sun, and I immediately headed toward the order line, so that when he glanced up from his paper to look for me he would see me in line texting on my iPhone and think I had been there for a while. Great plan, but it didn't work. He looked up within one second of my arrival and knew exactly how late I was.

I still don't know why I should have felt guilty being a few minutes late. It's not as if I was punching a time clock for a paying job and after all, I did buy most of the coffees. I headed directly over to his table.

J : Hi Red, sorry I'm late. My first mid-term is on Tuesday, and I've been burning the midnight oil to get ready.

R : Coffee's ready, Jimmy.

J : Great uh… where?

R : At the counter, Jimmy. Just needs paying for.

J : Okee dokee then. Be right back.

R : Take your time, you're only ten minutes late.

J : Here we are then. Hope they're still hot. So, as I was say—

R : No need Jimmy. Let's not waste any more time.

J : Sorry, Red? Are you in rush then?

R : No, Jimmy, I'm just selective about how I waste my time.

J : Right, like on the Comedy Network where they say 'time well wasted.'

R : Not really, Jimmy, I seldom watch TV, except for hockey.

J : How about PBS?

R : Not even PBS, although I understand they have some great shows.

J : So why don't you watch them?

R : Guilt avoidance Jimmy.

J : Guilt?

R : Aye Jimmy. I never donate.

J : That's amazing. I can't believe you'd feel guilty about anything.

R : I don't Jimmy.

J : But you just—

R : I simply avoid guilt, Jimmy.

J : Right. So we're doing Damper, the Demoralizer, right?

R : Correct, Jimmy. Chapter 27.

J : Not to change your plans too much, but would you mind if we started with Damper's nemesis before we get into the details about the Demoralizer?

R : Why's that, Jimmy?

J : Well we seem to cut our discussions short on this one important person, who can so easily undo all the progress that our Miz-Manager have made, and I think I'd like to understand it better.

R : No problem, Jimmy. To start with, you need to
know how to recognize your nemesis.

J : What do we look for?

R : Behaviour, Jimmy. Be careful when you see people who are
courteous and respectful. That's the first sign of trouble.

J : Kind of like a scout tracking down his enemy or stalking his prey—

R : Not at all Jimmy. You really like to overdramatize, don't
you. Y'need to think more like a subtle Peeping Tom.

J : That sounds a bit sneaky, don't you think?

R : Absolutely, Jimmy.

J : OK, so we're looking for 'nice' people who are courteous and respectful. What else?

R : Positive attitude, Jimmy. But it's a lot more difficult to detect than just behaviour.

J : Why is that?

R : Behaviour is usually quite obvious, Jimmy, right from the start. But,
positive attitude is not as blatant as negative attitude, and it tends
to materialize more slowly as you get to know someone better.

J : Why do say that negative attitude is more blatant?

R : Y'see Jimmy, if someone is arrogant, sullen or scornful, it's written all
over them and it oozes out of them before you even meet them.

J : Now that you mention it.

R : On the other hand, Jimmy, if they are *Sagacious, Ingenuous* or *Industrious,* it could take weeks or months before this type of attitude gets
noticed, and most people don't really take them very seriously anyway.

J : Really?

R : It's so uncommon, Jimmy, that people don't expect it,
and often they don't believe it at first either.

J : Well…

R : Just think about it, Jimmy. When you greet someone and ask them how they are, how often do you hear
a response like, *'fantastic'* or even *'excellent?'*

J : Not very often, I guess.

R : Be very wary of anyone who replies, 'excellent, and how are you?'

J : Why is that?

R : It could either be a sign of positivism, Jimmy, or
hopefully it's just a *one-off* situation.

J : What do you mean by *one-off?*

R : Well, Jimmy, if they're heading off to Mexico the next
day, then it's just a temporary condition, and you know
they'll be back to normal as soon as they return.

J : So they're not a real threat then?

R : No, Jimmy. Y'see a positive attitude has to be proven over

time, and fortunately most people, even *Brillies,* are very
suspicious of anyone with a positive attitude.

J : So you're suggesting that they aren't as popular as we all think?

R : Not at first, Jimmy, but once they establish themselves, they can be very
dangerous, especially those with an attitude like *Sagacious Idealism.*

J : That sounds really, really dangerous.

R : You used too many reallys, Jimmy.

J : It's a hyperbole.

R : Not a very good one, Jimmy. I don't think you appreciate the gravity of having this type of nemesis around.
The damage they can do is easily underestimated.

J : Like the pine beetle?

R : We're not talking about music, Jimmy.

J : Not *The Beatles.* The little tiny beetles that kill thousands of pine trees each year in Alberta and BC.

R : Oh, those wee beasties, Jimmy. That's a brilliant analogy.

J : Thanks… I think. So what kind of damage are we talking about?

R : *Motivating,* Jimmy, and illegally smuggling *Visionary* perspectives into the workplace.

J : That's got to be at least a 3 or even 4 '*really*' bad thing, right?

R : Cute, Jimmy.

J : Is that like a bad brilliant?

R : Worse, Jimmy.

J : Figures. So are those the objectives of our nemesis?

R : No, Jimmy. Their actions are to *Motivate* their colleagues to meet
their *Visionary* goals and their objective is to create an atmosphere of *Satisfaction* and *Acclamation* where they can act freely
and where their goals can be realized in a *Positive* environment.

J : I can't even imagine how many '*reallys*' should pre-
cede the word dangerous for that one.

R : It deserves an eight, Jimmy, but don't do it.

J : Agreed. Perhaps we should have a look at how to prevent
these villains from destroying all of Damper's hard work.

R : Right, Jimmy. *Malicious Sardonicism* would be a good start.

J : Sounds very effective, but what if Damper doesn't have a
natural inclination towards this type of attitude?

R : Good point, Jimmy. It's true that this type of attitude is more common amongst our sadistic allies, and as we've already discussed, most
Mizzies have difficulty personally adopting a sadistic attitude.

J : So how do they make this attitude adjustment then?

R : Vicariously, Jimmy.

J : Through someone else who's malicious and sardonic?

R : Exactly, Jimmy. There's no need for *Mizzies* to always have to go
through a personal attitude adjustment to achieve their objectives.

J : Does this concept apply to all of our heroes?

R : Absolutely, Jimmy. Just get someone else to do it for you.

J : Isn't it better if Damper demonstrates the appropriate attitude to achieve the most desired results?

R : As I've already told you, Jimmy, even the most effective *Mizzies* can't demonstrate all eight behaviours.

J : Could be difficult to find volunteers, don't you think?

R : That's what conscription is for, Jimmy.

J : That may work for the military, but it's not very effective in the workplace.

R : Who's the boss, Jimmy?

J : You're going to force someone to be malicious and sardonic?

R : Not force, Jimmy. *Manipulate.*

J : Can you give me an example of how to do that?

R : Not now, Jimmy.

J : When?

R : Chapter 21, Jimmy.

J : Right. Let's see… where's my chapter list? Ah, *here* it is chapter 21: The Prevaricator. That's the last one, right?

R : Impatience is a virtue, Jimmy.

J : Good to know I have at least one virtue.

R : Trust me, Jimmy, you have more than one.

J : Can't wait to find out what they are. So have we covered Damper's attitude?

R : For now, Jimmy.

J : So what's next?

R : Strength, Jimmy. *Damper's* strength in any organization shines when she takes charge of workplace morale.

J : She's a big morale booster then is she?

R : That's hopeless, Jimmy.

J : Maybe for you, Red, but most people don't see morale as being hope…

R : Hopeless booster, Jimmy. *Damper's* objective is to create a *Derisive Miz-Environment,* where morale is essentially reduced to hopelessness.

J : So instead of being a morale booster, she's a hopeless booster?

R : Something like that, Jimmy.

J : Maybe she could start a booster club.

R : Well, Jimmy, if she earns enough *Disrespect,* she'll soon have her own fan club.

J : Shouldn't that be a derision club?

R : Precisely, Jimmy.

J : I can imagine their meetings would be one endless party.

R : Not really, Jimmy, they should be held in an atmosphere of *Humiliation* and *Deprecation,* in keeping with the mood.

J : Sign me up.

R : You don't sound too sincere there, Jimmy.

J : You're right. It's not really my cup of tea.

R : That's *Arrogance,* Jimmy.

J : You think I'm arrogant because I don't want to join the hopeless club. Maybe I should join and moon them all to add to their humiliation and deprecation.

R : And *Disreputable* as well, that's fantastic, Jimmy.

J : I must be lost again.

R : Not at all, Jimmy. That's exactly the type of behaviour that *Damper* has to emulate.

J : What is?

R : Being Arrogant and Disreputable, Jimmy.

J : I wasn't being that arrogant, and I only talked about disreputable behaviour, I didn't do anything.

R : It's a start, Jimmy.

J : I can see how arrogance could be demoralizing, but how does being disreputable contribute to creating a derisive environment?

R : Someone has to set an example, Jimmy.

J : Fair enough.

R : But, you are right about *Arrogance,* Jimmy. It is a very powerful force, as long as you don't overdo it.

J : Can you ever have too much arrogance then?

R : Some people think that taking down the Titanic was a bit over the top.

J : C'mon Red. No one *took down* the Titanic. It was a series of unfortunate circumstances.

R : No, Jimmy. It was *Arrogance.*

J : Whose arrogance are we talking about?

R : The owners for one, Jimmy. But there was also a collective *Arrogance* that contributed to the disbelief that the Titanic was indestructible.

J : How did believing it was indestructible help take it down?

R : Inaction, Jimmy, or at lease delayed reaction… not enough life boats, no need for binoculars in the crow's nest, speeding in dangerous waters, ignoring warnings, no need for emergency plans and the like.

J : It was the iceberg that did it, Red.

R : Could have been avoided, Jimmy, if there were fewer or no arrogant people running the ship. However, it did provide an opportunity for some survivors to enjoy virtually endless *Mizery.*

J : How so?

R : Many of the men who boarded the life boats when there were still women and children on board earned a lifetime of *Disrespect* and perpetual *Mizery.*

J : You're right. It certainly can be powerful, if used carefully, but do you really think that any of those people were Mizzies?

R : That's not the point, Jimmy. These are example behaviours that *Damper* can try to emulate to create an effective *Derisive* environment.

J : OK, maybe you could help us understand how to do that?

R : You probably mean *High Sticking,* Jimmy.

J : Damper's hockey penalty secret code.

R :   That's H-U-B Jimmy.

J :   I take it that HUB is striking an opponent while carrying the stick above shoulder level, right?

R :   Right, Jimmy.

J :   And HUB stands for?

R :   Humiliating, Undermining, and Berating, Jimmy.

J :   With arrogance?

R :   Great, Jimmy. You turned your ears back on.

J :   So those are the behavioural practices; what are the goals and objectives?

R :   We already covered *Dampers* objective, Jimmy.

J :   Uh… Derisive?

R :   Right, Jimmy, and to get there, we start with our offensive actions: *Demean, Emasculate,* and *Disappoint.*

J :   Let me guess, it causes staff to feel demeaned, emasculated, and disappointed.

R :   Another good guess, Jimmy. You may not be hopeless after all.

J :   Does that mean no fan club then?

R :   Not at all, Jimmy. It would be filled with fans who are *Helpless, Ineffectual, Discouraged,* and *Vulnerable.*

J :   I'm humbled.

R :   Perhaps, Jimmy, but not *Humiliated.*

J :   I thought humility was a positive virtue?

R :   *Damper* is not the one being *Humiliated,* Jimmy.

J :   And by humiliating staff, they will be miserable, which will influence others to be miserable as well.

R :   That's the plan, Jimmy, and the more witnesses to the humiliation the greater the *Mizery.*

J :   Are we talking about publicly humiliating people, to send a message?

R :   That's it exactly, Jimmy.

J :   Kind of like public lashings on the old pirate ships then?

R :   Perhaps not so physical, Jimmy. In today's world *Mizzies* have to be creative to inflict mental anguish, not physical suffering.

J :   Like?

R :   Like parking tickets instead of pink slips, Jimmy.

J :   I'm not sure I understand that one.

R :   When downsizing, what is the more traditional way of firing people, Jimmy?

J :   Handing them their pink slips?

R :   Exactly, Jimmy. A few years back one company came up with an amazingly creative alternative. Instead of pink slips, the targeted staff were given parking tickets.

J :   How does that replace pink slips?

R :   Very effectively, Jimmy. Individually, they would return to the office in a huff and start complaining, which would attract a lot of attention. Then the manager would come out and ask what the problem was.

  The selected victim would complain louder about their parking ticket and then the manager would ask. "*Where were you parked?*" The victim would then, with increased frustration, reply. "*In my regular spot, where I always park.*" The manager would then nod in an understanding manner and say, "*Ah, there's the problem then. That spot is reserved for staff only.*"

J :   (Pause)

R :   That's a very strange look on your face, Jimmy. Do y'need to visit the wee laddies' room then?

J :   No, Red. I'm sure you mean that as a joke, but it's not very funny.

R :   It's just an example, Jimmy.

J :   An embarrassing one if it goes in the book.

R :   That's fantastic, Jimmy, Damper needs people to feel *Embarrassed*.

J :   Including me?

R :   Would you prefer *Degraded*, Jimmy?

J :   No.

R :   How about Diminished, Dissatisfied, Disillusioned, or Disturbed, Jimmy? Or maybe just Saddened?

J :   None; but I'm sure that won't stop you, and I'll bet you're just full of Miz-mms as well. Can we move on to our defence team then?

R :   Criticism, Jimmy.

J :   I'm not trying to be critical; I just don't want to be subjugated to all your D words and Miz-mms.

R :   Not you, Jimmy. It's *Damper* who needs to master the art of *Criticism*.

J :   Oh! Is that enough to counter a sagacious attitude?

R :   Well Jimmy, if you *Criticize Brillies* and *Offend* them on a regular basis, you make them feel *Censured* and *Offended*.

J :   Of course that doesn't work on me, because I'm so insensitive.

R :   It doesn't have to work on you, Jimmy. But it'll normally throw *Brillies* off balance, so they are less likely to impede *Damper* from achieving her objectives of creating an atmosphere of *Humiliation* and *Deprecation* within the bounds of a *Derisive Miz-Environment*.

J :   Is that all she has to do?

R :   She could try *Slighting* as well, but it might be wise to conscript some help to offset the impact of *Sagacious Idealism*.

J :   Don't you think that slighting is a bit of a lost art these days?

R :   It works on you, Jimmy.

J :   No comment. Is that it for our friend Damper?

R :   That's it, Jimmy.

J :   No fairy tale?

R :   Pinocchio, Jimmy.

J :   OK, so what's the story?

R :   Have you not read the book, Jimmy?

J :   Yeah, when I was a kid.

R :   It hasn't changed. Jimmy.

J :   What about your version?

R :   They're the same, Jimmy. Lessons in demoralization.

J :   That's it?

R :   Thanks for the coffee, Jimmy. See you next Saturday, same time; same place?

J :   Uh No. No, sorry Red, I have exams, so it will
have to be the following Saturday.

R :   No problem, Jimmy. Don't forget. Two weeks.
Whyte Avenue. 2:00 o'clock.

Once again there was no time to answer Red's question before he made it to the
door. Suddenly I felt slighted, and I realized that it did work on me. Damn.

Chapter 42

The Obstructer (Hamper)

I
Increase

Obstruct

To block, impede or hinder an action or operation

Even though it had only been two weeks since I last met with Red, it seemed like months. On this Saturday, following the final week of mid-terms, I should have been filled with exuberance, but I was not. I felt miserable even though I was sure that I had done well on most of my exams. The weather was unseasonably mild—which is why I didn't mention it—so that wasn't it either. I'd had a two week vacation from Mr. Red Knech, so that couldn't have been it either, unless… oh right, I had a meeting scheduled with Red Knech at 2:00 o'clock. That was it.

In between my studies and exams, I managed to find a little time to go through my notes, and I discovered, hidden between the disjointed reckonings of Mr. Knech, a pattern. I was truly amazed to find this unexpected consistency woven between the lines of my seemingly incomprehensible notes. It was such a genuine surprise that I felt like I had just discovered a treasure.

I immediately set up an Excel spread sheet to see if there really was some order amidst Red's apparently chaotic reckonings. Could I really unravel the mysteries of the Reckonings of Red Knech? When it actually worked, I was shocked. At first I couldn't wait to show it to Red, but now I was really nervous because I didn't know how he might react. What if I had it all wrong? With that negative thought consuming my mind with doubt, I headed off to the Second Cup on White Avenue. I was not surprised to see Red sitting there reading the Sun.

J : Hi, Red. Good to see you again.

R : It's been a while, Jimmy. How were the exams then?

J : I think I did OK. Coffee, Red?

R : Thanks, Jimmy. That would be great.

J : OK. I'll be right back.
    Here we go.

R : Thanks, Jimmy

J : I've got something to show you.

R : What's that then, Jimmy?

J : I know you think I don't always listen very well, but here it is. As you can see, I have been taking good notes. I charted out each of the eight behaviours and organized all the different characteristics, goals, objectives—

R : Wait a minute, Jimmy. What are you trying to do, ruin it?

J : Well no, I was just trying to make it easier—

R : No. No. No, Jimmy. We don't want to make it easy for them.
    Mizzies will be expecting us to understand their needs.

J : With all due respect, Red, we need to organize the flow of information—

R : No, Jimmy. We don't. You've got it all wrong. Our *Mizzie* readers will do that for themselves. If we include something like this in the book, we'll be depriving them of the *Miz-Experience* of suffering through the tedious task of doing it themselves.

J : Ya, but Red it's—

R : It's not going t'happen, Jimmy. That's the type of thing that those self-help books do to impress people, and then they repeat everything at the end of each chapter to make the book bigger.

J :   We could also add a few blank pages in the back and call them worksheets.

R :   Good idea, Jimmy, if someone else is paying for the publishing.

J :   OK. You've made your point. Should we get started on the Obstructer?

R :   Right, Jimmy. We don't want to hamper our progress.

J :   That's a good play on words, Red. I think you're loosening up a bit.

R :   Slip of the tongue, Jimmy.

J :   But the Obstructer's common name is Hamper, correct?

R :   Quite correct, Jimmy. Clearly best suited for financial management responsibilities.

J :   An accountant then?

R :   Preferably not, Jimmy. They're too organized. Accountants make much better *Dumbpers* or *Dampers* than *Hampers*.

J :   So what kinds of mizzies are best suited to be Obstructers then?

R :   Insecure *Mizzies,* Jimmy. *Hampers* are advantaged by the qualities of insecurity.

J :   How's that?

R :   They seem to have an insatiably unconscious desire to prove themselves, Jimmy.

J :   At what?

R :   *Mizery,* Jimmy. What else would it be?

J :   Of course. What else? Should we move on to *Hampers* behaviours?

R :   *Disloyal* and *Obnoxious,* Jimmy.

J :   All the obstructer types that I've ever run across have been obnoxious, so I get that one, but how does being disloyal help Hamper to achieve her goals and objectives?

R :   That's easy, Jimmy. Loyalty means supporting the best interests of the organization, so anyone who is loyal would not willingly obstruct any activity that might bring a ray of *Mizery* into the workplace.

J :   When you put it that way, disloyalty sounds a bit like being a spy.

R :   She's not Mata Hari, Jimmy.

J :   Might be a bit more exiting though.

R :   Am I boring you then, Jimmy?

J :   No. Of course not.

R :   Pity, Jimmy. That means we have to create a lot more tedium before we can wrap it up today.

J :   We have to reach our quota, don't we? What about the hockey penalty behavioural practice then?

R :   *Boarding,* Jimmy.

J :   No, I'm not bored again—

R :   Not bored again, Jimmy – *Boarding.*

J :   Oh, *that* hockey penalty. Shoving an opponent so that he is thrown violently against the boards.

R :   That's the one, Jimmy.

J :   What does Hamper have to practice then?

R : SOB Jimmy.

J : I presume it doesn't stand for Son of… some B word?

R : Correct Jimmy. It's *Stultifying, Obstructing,* and *Belittling.*

J : SOB eh? We might get letters on that one.

R : No problem, Jimmy. Just don't read them.

J : OK. I'll pretend they don't even exist.

R : That's the right *Nihilistic* spirit, Jimmy

J : Nihilism is the right spirit?

R : It is for *Hamper, Jimmy,* along with a *Supercilious* attitude.

J : Wow. A double threat.

R : Indeed, Jimmy. But she also has to learn to proficiently *Constrain, Impede,* and *Ridicule.*

J : Basic skill sets for Hamper, I presume.

R : And very important skills, Jimmy, especially if she wants to cause her staff to feel *Unappreciated, Restrained, Constricted,* and *Limited.*

J : Any constrained advice for Hamper on how to do this?

R : Freedom first, Jimmy.

J : Freedom for?

R : For staff, Jimmy. First she has to encourage her staff to take risks, be creative, submit new ideas and feel free to offer suggestions for improvement.

J : That doesn't sound very constraining.

R : Not right away, Jimmy. First they need a taste of freedom to maximize the *Miz-Effects* of *Constraint* when freedom of expression is rescinded and undermined.

J : Hamper giveth and Hamper taketh away.

R : Quite so, Jimmy. Build them up, then let them down hard. This also offers *Hamper* an opportunity to *Belittle* as well as *Constrain.*

J : Excellent, a two for one sale.

R : Half price, Jimmy. Suppose *Hamper* hands out assignments to several inexperienced, but promising *Brillies* in her group. She makes sure they don't have all the right information, so they can't accidentally do a good job and she also gives them a lot of latitude to be creative and try new methods or whatever.

J : For which, I presume, they will pay dearly.

R : You presume correctly, Jimmy. So when the assignments are completed, *Hamper* selects the absolutely worst one and proceeds to criticize it in front of everyone.

J : Isn't that something that Damper should be doing?

R : *Hamper* and *Damper* are partners, Jimmy. The point is that now she has reason to put serious constraints on everyone by declaring that this assignment was abysmal, and yet it was "the best of the lot", even though it really was the worst.

J : Does she have to go over the reasons why the others were apparently appalling as well, even though they were all better?

R : No need, Jimmy. If one apple is bad, then by association, they're all bad.

J : Even if some might actually have been done very well?

R : Especially then, Jimmy. That's the beauty of it. Now, without any justification, she can publically declare in one fell swoop, that all assignments failed *Mizerably*.

J : Bring on the constraints.

R : Absolutely, Jimmy, and then she can also ensure that the producer of the worst assignment is publicly *Ridiculed* and *Scorned*. The rest will feel *Mocked* and *Derided* by association.

J : Job well done.

R : Indeed, Jimmy.

J : Now she has them constrained and ridiculed as well, all she has to do is impede, is that right?

R : Just so, Jimmy, and that's usually quite easy. All she has to do is hold up approvals, and send out every document for review by as many people as possible.

J : I think that's actually policy in most publicly managed organizations.

R : Did you actually learn something at University, Jimmy?

J : No. I think I learned it from you.

R : Must be true then, Jimmy. If *Hamper* can learn as well, and set up a sufficiently complex and unmanageable approval processes, procedures, and protocols that require signatures from people who are never around, then her people will soon feel completely *Encumbered, Obstructed, Hindered,* and *Hampered*.

J : Time to bring on more Miz-mms.

R : There can never be enough *Miz-mms,* Jimmy.

J : Is that it for offence?

R : Aye, Jimmy, I think you've earned another coffee.

J : Good idea. What if I get it this time?

R : Well all right then, Jimmy. I'll keep our table.

J : OK, here we are.

R : Thanks, Jimmy, most appreciated.

J : Before we move on to defence, could we have a look at Hamper's nemesis?

R : If you like, Jimmy?

J : It would be good to know who we're dealing with.

R : *Industrious Pragmatism,* Jimmy.

J : Sound terrifying.

R : Even *Boarding* isn't always enough, Jimmy, which is why *Hamper* has to learn to master the art of *Inhibiting* and *Contradicting*.

J : Are we discussing defence now?

R : No, Jimmy. You asked me to describe *Hamper's* nemesis first.

J : Right. Industrious Pragmatism?

R : That's the attitude, Jimmy.

J : I don't think so, Red, I'm neither of—

R : Not you, Jimmy. You always seem to assume I'm talking about you. This is not about you.

J : Sorry, Red.

R : Y'know, Jimmy, there is help available for people like you.

J : I don't need that kind of help.

R : Good, Jimmy. Then if it's all right with you, could you please stay on track?

J : I'm good.

R : As I was saying, Jimmy, *Industrious Pragmatism* is the attitude that *Hamper* needs to defend against.

J : Does our nemesis have a recognizable behaviour?

R : Usually, Jimmy, they are very *Loyal* and highly *Supportive* of the organization.

J : That means trouble.

R : What that means, Jimmy, is that they are like self-appointed auditors, who keep an unofficial eye on how well everyone is serving the best interests of the organization.

J : Including watching Hamper?

R : Including *Hamper,* Jimmy, and that's the problem. This is why *Hamper* needs to build a strong defence against their objective.

J : What is their objective?

R : To create a *Permissive* environment, Jimmy, with an atmosphere of *Realization* and *Perception*.

J : No kidding, Red. Hamper sure can't afford to have any perceptive peeping toms around, who might figure out what she's doing.

R : Definitely not, Jimmy. This is why she has to defend against their diabolically *Constructive* and *Industrious* goals.

J : Do you have any examples to watch out for?

R : Real Streamlining and Process Busting, Jimmy.

J : What do you mean by real?

R : Well Jimmy, there are all kinds of supporters for the concept of continuous improvement, but most only pay lip service to the program. They don't really care if things improve or not; they only care about how they are personally perceived, to advance their careers.

J : You mean like those pseudo progressive phoneys, who—

R : That's brilliant, Jimmy. Another type of P^3.

J : So it is. How cleaver of me. I almost forgot that pseudo starts with a 'P.'

R : Don't worry, Jimmy. You're not the only one who has trouble with words that are pronounced with an 'S,' but are spelled with a 'P.'

J : Like Psycho?

R : Or pseudonym, psychedelic, psychiatry, and psychic, Jimmy.

J : Good to know. Maybe we should get back to Hamper's defence.

R : Quite right, Jimmy. She needs to *Inhibit* and to *Contradict* her nemesis for them to be *Restricted* and *Obstinate*.

J : How can you make someone become obstinate?

R : It's quite easy, Jimmy. What do we know about *Hamper's* nemesis?

J : Well they are loyal, supportive, industrious, pragmatic, constructive, and industrious.

R : Exactly, Jimmy, which makes them very determined people.

J : So?

R : And so, Jimmy, what other characteristic behaviour is so often associated with determined people?

J : No idea.

R : Stubbornness, Jimmy.

J : And that makes them obstinate?

R : Usually, Jimmy. The more you can obstruct them from achieving their goals and objectives, the more determined and stubborn they become.

J : How does that help?

R : It keeps them focused on their sandcastles, Jimmy.

J : How did we get to sandcastles all of a sudden?

R : The nemesis' objectives are like sandcastles, Jimmy.

J : You mean they're wet and soggy.

R : No, Jimmy.

J : Do they have layers like onions?

R : Why would they have layers Jimmy?

J : Ogres have layers.

R : What have Ogres got to do with sandcastles?

J : Well Shrek has layers.

R : Who the hell is Shrek, Jimmy, and what are on about now?

J : Oh, I felt for a moment there that I was caught inside a Shrek movie and…

R : (Pause)

J : Right, you've never seen a Shrek movie have you?

R : No, Jimmy.

J : OK, I'm sorry! So how are these achievements like sandcastles anyway?

R : Just when they think they've been achieved, *Hamper's* wave of *Inhibition* and *Contradiction* rolls in and wipes them out, so they have to start all over again. And with that, Hamper can create an atmosphere of *Debilitation* and *Exacerbation* in a *Restrictive Miz-Environment*.

J : That's all?

R : It is, Jimmy. I'm off now, and I'll see you at 2 o'clock, over at Telus on Tuesday, if you think you can be a little less obnoxious.

J : What about the Skit?

R : Have a read of the Valiant Little Tailor, Jimmy, and take note of how cleverly he obstructs his enemies.

With those words trailing behind him as he stormed out of the coffee shop, I silently sat there repressing a smile on my face. I think I finally gave Red a bit of his own back and it was clear that he couldn't take it very well. Then the guilt slowly started to set in. I hadn't really intended to offend him, but this wasn't the first time during one of our sessions that I felt as if I was being drawn into some surreal or comic movie. The fact that his manner of speech reminded me so much of Mike Myers doing his Shrek voice just drew me in further.

Well, that was enough guilt for one day. It was time to go home.

Chapter 17

The Equivocator
(Stupor)

Sui
Following

Equivocate

To use equivocal language intentionally, to speak in ambiguities

As much as I hate waiting for a bus in winter, I assumed that it would be easier than trying to find inexpensive parking downtown. I was wrong. I nearly froze my fingers waiting for the bus that would take me to the LRT, and then I nearly froze my toes as well as I waited again for the train. The thought of having to repeat this process on the return trip back, with an additional stop at the University to visit with my thesis advisor made me concede to the probability that I really must be a Mizzy—as is *anyone* else who stays here during winter.

This time, when I reached the underground urban maze, I raced all the way to Telus Plaza trying desperately to warm up. As I approached Second Cup, I spotted Red snuggled up beside the fake fireplace, and I scurried towards him rubbing my hands together coaching some meagre amounts of warmth from friction. As I stood beside Red, tapping my toes and blowing on my hands, Red didn't even look up from his paper.

J : Hi, Red.
R : New dance step there, Jimmy?
J : No. Just cold. Where's your coffee?
R : Daryl's not here today, so I had to wait for you Jimmy.
J : Good thing I'm not late then.
R : I'd have ordered myself, but I didn't want to lose this seat.
J : Good plan, Red. It might help me warm up.
R : Coffee helps too, Jimmy.
J : Right. I'll just dump my stuff and go get us some coffee.
R : Muffin would be nice too, Jimmy.
J : Got it.
R : Thanks, Jimmy.
J : No problem there Red, but I do have a problem with time today.
R : How come, Jimmy?
J : Unfortunately, I have a meeting with my thesis advisor at 3:00, so I only have about a half hour.
R : Best not waste any time then, Jimmy.
J : Right. I've got my checklist here, which should speed—
R : I thought we weren't going to use that, Jimmy?
J : Maybe not in the book Red, but it's really more like a list of questions, so we can get through this faster.
R : OK fine, Jimmy. Get to it then.
J : All right, according to my notes, we should be discussing Chapter 17: The Equivocator, whose common name is...?
R : *Stupor,* Jimmy.
J : Great. And he manages what?
R : *Production,* Jimmy.
J : What's his behaviour?
R : *Her* behaviour, Jimmy, is being *Disorganized* and *Indecisive.*
J : What about behavioural practices then?
R : *VCR* Jimmy.

J :   Meaning?

R :   *Tripping* Jimmy.

J :   Ah, the hockey penalty. Using a stick, knee, foot, arm, hand, or elbow to cause an opponent to trip or fall.

R :   You did come prepared, Jimmy.

J :   Easy guess. There aren't that many hockey penalties left. So what does VCR stand for?

R :   *Vacillating, Confounding,* and *Rambling,* Jimmy.

J :   With offence actions to?

R :   *Confuse, Confound,* and *Distract,* Jimmy.

J :   And the goal is to cause people to be?

R :   *Confused,* Jimmy, as well as *Disorganized, Disordered, Incompetent,* and *Disarranged.*

J :   That should be easy. What else?

R :   *Distracted, Unproductive, Inefficient, Unfocused,* and *Preoccupied,* Jimmy.

J :   What about confounded?

R :   Same as *Baffled,* Jimmy, but also *Bewildered, Perplexed,* and *Puzzled.*

J :   Fantastic, three goals in less than 10 minutes. At this rate we'll be done in less than half an hour.

R :   Does that mean only one coffee, Jimmy?

J :   Probably for me, Red, but don't worry, I'll get you a refill before I leave.

R :   Fine, Jimmy. Keep going then.

J :   So tripping is fuelled by an attitude of what?

R :   *Fallacious Syndicalism,* Jimmy.

J :   We've already discussed syndicalism, so I think I know where you're going on this. Are the red light signs still Miz-mms?

R :   Definitely, Jimmy, and you seem to know them all.

J :   Is there a Miz-atmospheric objective?

R :   There is, Jimmy. An atmosphere of *Disorganization* and *Vacillation.*

J :   Something that I'm quite familiar with these days.

R :   More progress then, Jimmy.

J :   OK then, what about defence?

R :   To *Befuddle* and *Shilly-shally,* Jimmy.

J :   Is shilly-shally a real word?

R :   It is, Jimmy.

J :   Good, because I feel like that a lot lately, and it's important to know that it's a real word. And the defence goal is to cause Brillies to be *what*?

R :   Feel *Disorganized* and *Incompetent,* Jimmy.

J :   Some folks might mistake them for P³s then?

R :   Maybe, Jimmy, but they'll still be perceived with *Derision.*

J :   In a heavenly Miz-environment no doubt?

R :   A *Divisive* environment, Jimmy.

J :   Amazing. We have two more goals in record time and a divisive environment to enjoy our Miz-success.

R :   You're on a roll there, Jimmy, unless you run into your nemesis.

J : Right, and what's he up to?

R : Aside from being *Organized* and *Decisive*, Jimmy, he's a stubborn one.

J : And what will he try to do to reach his goal that must be thwarted?

R : Stay *Focused* and be *Decisive*, Jimmy.

J : Fuelled, no doubt, by a subversive attitude?

R : *Duteous Devotion*, Jimmy.

J : And all this duteous devotion is striving to create an atmosphere of what?

R : *Organization* and *Resolution*, Jimmy.

J : Leading to?

R : A *Cooperative* Environment, Jimmy.

J : Is that it for the equivocator then?

R : That's it, Jimmy, all except for the skit.

J : And what fairy tale do we have this time?

R : *The Wonderful Wizard of Oz*, Jimmy.

J : Do we really need it?

R : Your impatience is showing, Jimmy.

J : Really? We got through that in record time, and I still have 10 minutes left.

R : Lucky for you, Jimmy. You've got time for another question then.

J : OK. What's the connection to the Wizard of Oz?

R : Like the Wizard, Jimmy, *Stupor* often finds herself in a situation where it is necessary to resort to using equivocal language and be-haviour to ensure that people will do her bidding. She can't afford to be honest with them, or they won't complete their assignments.

J : You mean like lying to Dorothy about being able to take her back to Kansas if she killed the wicked witch?

R : That, Jimmy, and the part about the witch being wick-ed when she was just a little bit upset—and green.

J : Green and upset?

R : Of course, Jimmy. Wouldn't you be upset if a house just fell on your sister?

J : You saw the musical, *Wicked*, didn't you?

R : The real story, Jimmy. Y'see how easy it was to create an ef-fective *Miz-Environment* for an innocent green child.

J : But the Wizard of Oz wasn't even in that play.

R : No, Jimmy. But he's still an excellent role model for *Stupor*, as is Glenda.

J : Are we done with Stupor then?

R : For now, Jimmy.

J : Good, 'cause I have to have a chat with my thesis advisor.

R : That could be positively *Mizerable*, Jimmy, if you play your cards right.

J : What do you mean?

R : Universities, Jimmy, are the perfect spawning grounds for proliferating effective *Miz-Environments*.

J : Why would you say that?

R : Tenure, Jimmy.

J : How can tenure possibly contribute to creating a Miz-environment?

R : It's a potential haven for *Part-time Mizzies*, Jimmy.

J :   Now we have part-time Mizzies? I suppose I have to ask you what they are.

R :   They're a bit similar to *Mini-Mizzies,* Jimmy, except they switch back and forth from being *Mizzies* for a while, then to *Non-Mizzies* and back again.

J :   Like alternating current or weekend warriors?

R :   Not quite so quick in their turn around, Jimmy. More like snow birds you know. Six months on and six months off.

J :   So what has tenure got to do with these part-timers?

R :   When you can't be fired, Jimmy, you pretty much have free reign to do whatever you want.

J :   Profs are very responsible people, and they would never abuse this right.

R :   I believe that's true for most Profs, Jimmy. The majority use this special privilege responsibly and ethically, but there are always a few that take advantage of their situation and demonstrate the potential of tenure to contribute to creating a perfectly marvellous *Miz-Environment.*

J :   For example?

R :   If *Stupor* happens to be a Prof, Jimmy, she could learn how to take advantage of her grad students. She could get them to do all the work on a research program and then put her own name on the publication, without having to do any of the work.

J :   By not doing work, isn't she missing out on a Miz-Experience.

R :   Not if she *likes* doing work, Jimmy.

J :   But wouldn't it be a bit unethical to get her students to do her job?

R :   What's your point, Jimmy?

J :   Wouldn't she at least have to review the paper and edit it before it gets published?

R :   If you say so, Jimmy. You know the University better than I do. But she might also learn how to persuade a grad student to teach all her classes for her, or prepare exams and grade all the test papers, so she can go to conferences.

J :   Profs have a lot of commitments and sometimes need help with some of these things.

R :   For which they get well compensated, Jimmy. But if *Stupor* elected not to share the compensation fairly with her students, the students would have little recourse and this could contribute quite nicely to a short term *Miz-Environment.*

J :   I think you're way off base there, Red.

R :   Probably, Jimmy. But you can always put it to the test.

J :   In what way?

R :   Try challenging your thesis advisor, Jimmy. Take a hard line position in opposition to every suggestion she offers and anything she insists that you do.

J :   That would be really rude, and she'd just think I was being a jerk.

R :   Even if you were right, Jimmy?

J :   She's the Prof, Red. I'm only a student.

R :   Exactly, Jimmy. But if you really knew you were right

	and you held your ground, what would happen?
J :	She'd probably flunk me.
R :	No doubt, Jimmy, and you'd have to just accept it, because she is protected by tenure and you have no recourse.
J :	I don't really see anything wrong with that.
R :	Absolutely nothing wrong with it, Jimmy. All I'm saying here is that this is a great example of a situational opportunity for *Stupor* to use to her advantage when creating a short term *Miz-Environment,* just the way the Wizard of Oz took advantage of his situation.
J :	I don't see the similarity there?
R :	Simple, Jimmy. The Emerald City gave the Wizard tenure. They gave him an ivory tower, let him do whatever he wanted to do and guaranteed never to fire him. So he took advantage of this opportunity.
J :	Great. Sorry I have to run, Red, but I don't want to be late.
R :	Next Tuesday, same time and same place, Jimmy? Don't forget my coffee then.
J :	Fine. See you then.

With that I quickly bought a coffee for Red, grabbed my stuff and scooted toward the LRT as fast as I could. I was so tempted to glance back to see what the expression was on Red's face. I was trying to imagine how startled he might be when I had bolted away from our session, just the way he did after each of our previous meetings. Then suddenly it occurred to me how disappointed I'd be if he wasn't at all fazed by my actions. There was no looking back. I preferred to believe the image in my imagination and avoid any more disappointment.

I slowed to a fast pace as I approached the escalator down to the platform, and as I stood there catching my breath, I began to feel a bit foolish. I realized that there was absolutely no point in trying to do to Red what he does to others. Spiders and snakes are always immune to their own venom.

Chapter 21

The Prevaricator
(Duper)

Shih Ho
Biting Through

Prevaricate

To stray from or evade the truth, to walk crookedly, deviate from one's course

Perhaps it was because Christmas was so close that Telus Plaza seemed so festive. Then again it may have been because this was my final session with the ubiquitous Mr. Red Knech. Even though Christmas was still almost a week away, my anticipation for the completion of these coffee sessions made me feel more elated than I normally do on Christmas morning. After all, we only had to finish this one last behaviour and it would be over… or would it?

Red was normally very unpredictable, except for one thing… his coffee. True to form, he occupied his favourite seat by the fake fireplace with coffee and muffin in hand.

J : Afternoon, Red.
R : Ah Jimmy. Daryl's expecting you.
J : Really? It's so nice to know that someone wants to see me.
R : He just wants your money, Jimmy.
J : No surprise there. I'll go get my coffee, pay for yours, and be right back.
R : No rush, Jimmy.
J : Fresh hot coffee really warms you up on a cold day.
R : As does the fireplace, Jimmy.
J : But it's not the same as a real wood fireplace.
R : Don't look at it then, Jimmy. Just enjoy the heat and pretend.
J : OK. So last chapter?
R : Is that a question, Jimmy?
J : Uh no, I don't suppose—
R : Then let's get on with it, Jimmy.
J : So it's Duper: The Prevaricator, right?
R : It is, Jimmy. She would be best suited to be in charge of ethics management, if she had the choice.
J : Could you tell me a bit about her special code of behaviour then?
R : That would be *Unreliable* and *Dishonest*, Jimmy.
J : Why would it be unreliable and dishonest of you to tell me, is there something unethical about it?
R : Yes… it wouldn't, Jimmy?
J : What is that supposed to mean?
R : '*Yes*' to your second question, Jimmy, and '*it wouldn't*' to your first.
J : You know, Red, I thought my exams were confusing, but your tests are just plain weird.
R : What tests are you on about, Jimmy? I simply answered your question.
J : I'm sorry, I must have missed the answer.
R : Another mini-skirt was it, Jimmy?
J : Yeah, that must have been it.
R : *Unreliable* and *Dishonest* are *Duper's* behavioural trademarks, Jimmy. And, yes, sometimes she may be just a tiny bit unethical.
J : Of course. How else could she qualify for the job?
R : How indeed, Jimmy?
J : So what does she practice then?

R : T-L-C Jimmy?

J : Are you sure? That doesn't sound so unethical.

R : It's definitely TLC, Jimmy.

J : Tender love and care? I—

R : That's brilliant, Jimmy. I'll have to remember that.

J : Remember what?

R : Tender love and care, Jimmy. That's also TLC.

J : But you just said… never mind. OK, so how does the Prevaricator use tender love and care to perpetuate change?

R : She doesn't, Jimmy.

J : She doesn't? What are the techniques then?

R : You must have a memory problem, Jimmy. I've already told you, it's TLC.

J : You mean T-L-C, Tender Love and Care?

R : No, Jimmy, and you're repeating yourself again. Tender Love and Care has nothing at all to do with *Trying, Lying,* and *Conniving.*

J : Trying, lying, and conniving?

R : Aye, Jimmy, I just said that.

J : Not Tender Love and Care then?

R : No, Jimmy, but I really like that one, and I promise to remember it.

J : If you like it, it's yours, OK? If you really promise to remember.

R : Thanks very much, Jimmy. I keep my promises, but *Duper* never does.

J : So even if Duper knew about Tender Love and Care, she wouldn't keep her promises.

R : Never, Jimmy. Now, are we straight on what TLC means?

J : I think so, but why doesn't Duper ever keep her promises?

R : So she can practice TLC, Jimmy.

J : Any examples?

R : When she hires someone, Jimmy, she makes all kinds of promises, but never puts them in writing.

J : Such as?

R : Simple things, Jimmy, like a promise to give them a $10,000 raise after the first year if they do a good job.

J : That seems reasonable.

R : Not if she doesn't honour her commitment, unless of course the employee is a *Mizzy.*

J : If confronted by the employee, how does she deny the promise with a straight face?

R : Easy, Jimmy. She just says, 'Sorry, I don't know anything about that.'

J : What if the employee reminds her of the interview?

R : Simply reply with a question, Jimmy: 'Who interviewed you?'

J : So what's the real objective here?

R : That's the best part, Jimmy. If the employee is a *Brillie,* he or she will likely quit, which gets rid of one more problematic *Brillie.*

J : And if he stays, it's probably because he is already a Mizzy.

R : That's it, Jimmy.

J :   Very effective way of weeding out the *Brillies*.

R :   Indeed, Jimmy. Another good one is overtime.

J :   I hate to break it to you, Red, but lots of people work overtime.

R :   True, Jimmy. But the trick is to make them work really late past midnight so they'll be late coming in the next morning.

J :   They need at least a few hours' sleep.

R :   They do, Jimmy, and so does the *Duper*, who stayed up with them.

J :   So she would understand why they would come in late, would she not?

R :   Of course, Jimmy, *Duper* might, but *Duper's* boss might not.

J :   Wouldn't Duper have informed her boss that her folks were working all... Oh Right... I get it. She wouldn't, would she?

R :   Of course not, Jimmy. That way, her ignorant boss can yell at them for being late, and if they are *Brillies*, they'll likely quit.

J :   Mission accomplished. Well I can see how this lying and conniving might cause some frustration, but what's a good example of trying?

R :   You, Jimmy.

J :   I am? What am I trying to do?

R :   Apparently nothing, Jimmy. But right now you are very trying.

J :   Ah! You mean trying, as in *annoying*; very funny.

R :   Finally, Jimmy. Perhaps there's a light on in there somewhere after all.

J :   Are there more ways of being trying?

R :   There are, Jimmy.
(Long pause)

J :   Are you going to share them with me?

R :   No, Jimmy.

J :   Now you're really, trying, aren't you?

R :   Exactly, Jimmy.

J :   Very effective.

R :   Isn't it just, Jimmy? Now, when it comes to trying, aside from the methods you use on me, there are—

J :   Wait a minute, I'm not trying to be trying.

R :   Maybe not, Jimmy, but for someone who's not trying you're very good at it.

J :   Not as good as you.

R :   As I was about to say before you interrupted me, Jimmy, there are a number of ways to be trying. You've already mastered the art of interruption, so I don't have to dwell on that one—

J :   I wasn't interrupting, I was—

R :   There! You did it again, Jimmy, and you did it very effectively as well.

J :   Sorry.

R :   Don't be, Jimmy. Y've just demonstrated one of the easiest methods of trying someone's patience. Another effective technique is to always be unavailable when your people need decisions, advice, direction, a signature for approval or basically anything.

J :   Sounds like she could use Harry Potter's invisible cloak.

R : A friend of yours Jimmy, this Harry fellow?

J : Not really, no. He's a character in a kid's book.

R : I don't think it will work anyway, Jimmy. It has to be quasi-legitimate invisibility.

J : Which means?

R : Conferences and meetings are the best, Jimmy. A good *Miz-Manager* can always fill her calendar with meetings, teleconferences, videoconferences, long lunches, lectures, training sessions and—most important—conferences and workshops far away from the workplace.

J : What if there is empty space on her calendar?

R : She just fills it up, Jimmy?

J : You mean she fakes it?

R : It's called creativity, Jimmy. An effective *Prevaricator* spends most of the day in unproductive meetings and then works hard in the evenings and on weekends to undo the damage done by *Virtuous* Brillies.

J : Virtuous Brillies?

R : Brillies with an attitude of *Virtuous Fanaticism,* Jimmy.

J : Oh, *those* guys.

R : So Jimmy, by being unavailable to respond to problems in the workplace, these unresolved issues will soon fester, and this will be very trying for everyone.

J : But sometimes the employees really like it when the manager is away from the office.

R : Excellent point, Jimmy, if the *Miz-Manager* is absent too much, the *Brillies* might take over the ship eh?

J : A mutiny then?

R : Indeed, Jimmy.

J : How can Duper prevent that?

R : Outsourcing, Jimmy.

J : You can't outsource just any activity. Sometimes there's no financial benefit to outsourcing certain tasks.

R : There's almost never a financial benefit to out-tasking anything, Jimmy.

J : Then why is it so widely used?

R : It's like housecleaning, Jimmy.

J : I'm almost afraid to ask, but why is it like housecleaning?

R : Aside from *Mizzies,* Jimmy, do you know of anyone who really likes housecleaning?

J : I suppose not.

R : So if money is not an issue, Jimmy, what do people do?

J : Hire a housekeeper?

R : Only *Mizzies* and P^3s do that, Jimmy.

J : What do you mean?

R : Finding, keeping, and managing the right housekeeper can generate as much if not more *Mizery* than doing it yourself if the housekeeper is managed according to the lessons learned in our book.

J :   So?

R :   Y'see, Jimmy, *Mizzies* appreciate suffering the consequences of their housekeepers always being late, not showing up, doing a poor job, quitting without notice, breaking things or even stealing stuff and the like.

J :   OK, that would definitely work for a Mizzy, but what do Brillies and P³s do?

R :   Outsource it to a company, Jimmy.

J :   I expect that costs more, but how does it help?

R :   Well, Jimmy, as you pointed out, it may be a tad more expensive, but it does offer reduced *Mizery* for *Brillies*. If there's a problem, they just phone the company and the problem gets resolved by someone else.

J :   But you just said that outsourcing was an option for Mizzies and P³s to use, and now you're saying it's also OK for Brillies?

R :   No, Jimmy. It's great, if you want to get rid of someone and you can't fire them.

J :   Really?

R :   Really, Jimmy. Sometime she just needs to get rid of these *Virtuous Fanatics*.

J :   How does she go about doing that, especially if these Brillies are recognized as top performers?

R :   Cross Checking, Jimmy.

J :   Ah, a little TLC then?

R :   Exactly, Jimmy. She just has to discredit her *Virtuous Brillie* and convince senior management that it would be in the best interest of the organization to outsource their respective responsibilities.

J :   Trying, lying, and conniving then?

R :   Not *Trying*, Jimmy. Just *Lying* and *Conniving* will do. For starters, she simply needs to *Miz-Spend, Miz-Appropriate, Miz-Place, Miz-Allocate* or *Miz-Approve* some funds that are under the responsibility of her *Virtuous Brillie* to demonstrate the incompetence and inefficiency of her nemesis.

J :   That sounds like framing or cooking the books.

R :   *Lying*, Jimmy. Next, she takes this information to senior management, along with a proposal to improve efficiency by outsourcing her *Virtuous Brillie's* entire group.

J :   Conniving, right?

R :   Very astute, Jimmy. Then she can force her *Virtuous Brillie* to retire with a modest settlement and outsource the work to some inefficient expensive company to ensure the *Miz-Continuance* of the operations.

J :   How can she ensure that it will go to an inefficient and inexpensive firm?

R :   Easy, Jimmy. Before her *Virtuous Brillie* departs, have him review the draft RFP and then make sure that none of his good advice is incorporated in it so there are numerous loopholes and pitfalls.

J :   OK, I'm lost again. First of all what's an RFP again?

R :   Did you forget chapter 24 already, Jimmy? It's a Request for Proposal, which is usually advertised in the newspaper so companies will submit a proposal to provide the services required.

J : But, why on earth would her nemesis even bother to look at this RFP? Isn't that a bit insulting?

R : It is indeed, Jimmy.

J : What makes you think he would provide advice on how to make sure the RFP is correct?

R : What kind of Brillie is he, Jimmy?

J : A virtuous fanatic?

R : Exactly, Jimmy, and probably ethical as well.

J : Definitely can't have people like that around, can we?

R : No place for them in a *Miz-Organization,* Jimmy. If she manages the RFP process correctly she will have successfully replaced a group of competent in-house workers with a much less
virtuous external manager, who is more interested in making
money than serving the best interests of the organization.

J : Well, as we know, work can get done without a virtuous manager, as long as the workers are not incompetent.

R : True, Jimmy, but there are always a few good P^3 workers in organizations that provide out-tasked services.

J : Is Duper accountable if she selects an inefficient firm then?

R : Not really, Jimmy. She just has to make sure that the panel members who
review the RFP have no experience in selecting outsourced services.

J : Before we got sidetracked on outsourcing, you were talking about the downside for Duper when she's not around
a lot. Does this make her vulnerable in any way?

R : Expendable, Jimmy, unless she has some allies or strong
supporters watching the shop when she's away.

J : To do what?

R : *Miz-Maintenance,* Jimmy.

J : An example might be helpful.

R : For you or the readers, Jimmy?

J : Me. I'm not really concerned about the readers anymore.

R : Why's that, Jimmy?

J : I think you were right when you suggested that many of our readers
won't make it this far, and those who do probably won't care either.

R : That's the spirit, Jimmy. Well there is this one *Miz-Myth* that I can think of.

J : Is that like an urban myth?

R : Exactly, Jimmy, but less believable. *Duper's* predecessor *Stupor* had
already created a highly *Miz-Effective Derisive* environment, so *Stupor*
decided to move her office to be right in the middle between the Big-
Endians on the north side and the Little-Endians on the south side.

J : I take it you are a fan of Jonathon Swift?

R : Indeed Jimmy. I only borrow from the best.

J : Why did she make this move?

R : To maximize her *Miz-Experience,* Jimmy.

J : I should have guessed.

R : Anyway, Jimmy, while she was away, the Little-Endians, who were all *Duteous* and *Devoted Brillies*, decided that they needed a separate identity and adopted the Confederate flag as their symbol.

J : Representing the south?

R : Symbolically, Jimmy. They proudly displayed a wee Confederate flag at each of their desks. So *Duper's* 1st Lieutenant, a Big-Endian by the name of Vik Timm, filed a discrimination charge against her, citing the flags as evidence of prejudice and her support for slavery.

J : There may be some twisted logic for filing a complaint against the Little-Endians, but why would Vik Timm file charges against Duper?

R : *Miz-Maintenance,* Jimmy. Vik's primary responsibility is to ensure that *Duper* experiences a constantly high level of *Mizery*. And in turn, Vik could expect to benefit by receiving his fair share of the resultant *Miz-Environment*.

J : Another win-win scenario then.

R : It should have been, Jimmy, but unfortunately the head of security noticed the flags and instructed *Duper* to order them removed. Apparently the company policy allows only the national flag or the company flag to be displayed in the office.

J : What a shame.

R : A real shame indeed, Jimmy, because our *Duteous* and *Devoted* Little-Endians took the order seriously and—

J : Wait a minute, Red, I thought that duteous and devoted were the characteristic traits of Stupor's nemesis?

R : They're interchangeable, Jimmy, and they were also *Virtuous Fanatics*.

J : Great, another double threat.

R : Double trouble indeed, Jimmy. So they sent a written signed apology to the head of security, acknowledging their sole responsibility for their actions, which inadvertently exonerated *Duper* completely.

J : That was a bit of rotten luck then.

R : Worse than that, Jimmy. Not only was this opportunity for an extensive amount of enviable *Mizery* snuffed out in a flash, but Vik was encouraged to leave the organization.

J : This may be an indelicate question, but… how can I put it…uh…?

R : Was Vik Timm Caucasian, Jimmy? Is that the question then?

J : Uh…yeah, that's it.

R : Not exactly, Jimmy, but his behaviour was very similar to that of the head of a certain White Supremacy Group.

J : You mean discrimination?

R : No, not really, Jimmy. Vik seemed to treat everyone with equal disdain, with the possible exception of one small group.

J : And who might that be?

R : Women, Jimmy. But that may not have been entirely his fault.

J : I don't think I want to know why?

R : It may have been a cultural thing, Jimmy.

J : OK, let's *definitely* not go there. I take it he wasn't a white supremacist then?

R : Unfortunately, Jimmy, after catching a peek at himself in the mirror one day, he realized he didn't physically qualify for membership.

J : And?

R : He started his own group, Jimmy.

J : Really? Did he have a lot of followers?

R : None, Jimmy.

J : Well at least he wouldn't have much dissension in his new group.

R : Not quite true, Jimmy.

J : How so?

R : He argued with himself a lot, Jimmy. And for some reason, he seemed to lose most of those arguments.

J : That's not good.

R : But worst of all, Jimmy, *Duper* was soon left without her 1st Lieutenant.

J : You just can't depend on those unpredictable Brillies.

R : Very true, Jimmy, which is why *Duper* must always keep her *Brillies* and their *Virtuous Fanaticism* in check to maintain an effective *Miz-Environment*.

J : Is that the cue for another hockey penalty?

R : What cue, Jimmy?

J : Checking?

R : *Cross checking*, Jimmy. We already did *Checking*.

J : Ah, right. The Tergiversator. I forgot.

R : It's not the same as *Cross Checking*, Jimmy.

J : I know. It's hitting an opponent with both hands on the stick.

R : Right, Jimmy. Did it take you a long time to memorize all the penalties then?

J : I don't remember. It was a long time ago.

R : What's a long time ago in your world, Jimmy?

J : I don't know, maybe ten or twelve years ago?

R : I suppose its all relative, Jimmy. That's a short time ago in my world.

J : What's a long time ago for you?

R : Before you were born, Jimmy.

J : That's long. So cross checking is the Mizzy code for the behavioural practice of TLC, is that correct?

R : Aye, Jimmy, quite correct. I take it you got a lot of penalties when you played hockey back then eh?

J : No, I didn't. So what must Duper do—

R : Were you that good then, Jimmy?

J : No, actually I spent a lot of time on the bench.

R : Attitude adjustment, Jimmy.

J : That didn't work. I was just too small and there was nothing wrong with my— wait a minute—you… you're not referring to me, are you?

R :   No, I'm not Jimmy.

J :   You almost got me, but I'm starting to catch on.

R :   Good thing we're almost done then, eh Jimmy?

J :   A very good thing. So what is this attitude adjustment for our friend Duper?

R :   *Mendacious Cynicism,* Jimmy. If you really are a serious movie buff, then you've probably seen Cat on a Hot
Tin Roof and you won't need your wee dictionary.

J :   I have seen it, and I don't need my dictionary, thank you very much.

R :   Good to hear, Jimmy.

J :   So what's our offence strategy?

R :   To *Frustrate*, is the first action, Jimmy.

J :   He shoots…he scores! One goal for you, Red.

R :   You seem *Frustrated*, Jimmy. Are you OK?

J :   Aside from feeling discouraged, impatient,
irked, strained and drained, I'm—

R :   Oh good, Jimmy. I thought for a minute there was something wrong.

J :   What's the next one?

R :   To *Dupe,* Jimmy.

J :   And the third one?

R :   To *Manipulate,* Jimmy. I—

J :   Hat trick!

R :   How so, Jimmy?

J :   You just scored three goals. You've managed to make me
feel completely frustrated, duped, and manipulated.

R :   We'd best be getting you a bit of tender love and care then, Jimmy?

J :   Too late. What I best be needing is a wee scotch before I expire.

R :   Is there a best before date there, Jimmy?

J :   I don't think alcohol has a best before date, Red.

R :   Best before marriage, Jimmy…
(pause)
Careful now, Jimmy. There's a hint of a wee smile peeking through that
stone face of yours. You take everything far too seriously. I don't believe
for one minute that you're really feeling *Pissed Off.* Nor are you affected
by any of the other synonyms, like *Deceived, Misinformed, Tricked, Double-
crossed, Cheated, Corrupted, Controlled, Misled, Conned,* or *Deluded.*

J :   Another coffee?

R :   Brilliant, Jimmy, and I don't mean your performance. I'll come up with you.

J :   I suppose this will be our last coffee for a while.

R :   Well Jimmy, at least until after the New Year anyway.

J :   I don't think we discussed Duper's defence?

R :   I think you are probably already familiar with *Tricking* and
Cheating, so we don't need to spend much time on that.

J :   I think we spent too much time on them already.

R :   Are you being *Dishonest* and *Deceitful*, Jimmy?

J :   Is that another trick question?

R :   Not really Jimmy. If you say *yes*, then defence goals have been met.

J :   If I say *no*?

R :   Then you'd be *Dishonest,* Jimmy, and I'd have to look upon you with *Deceit* and the defence goal would still be met.

J :   Great, a trick question with a win-win answer. What about the objective?

R :   An atmosphere of *Perversion* and *Corruption*, Jimmy, enveloped in a perfectly *Deceptive Miz-Environment.*

J :   Workplace paradise.

R :   Unless our nemesis brings on a snow storm, Jimmy.

J :   What might that look like?

R :   A *Supportive* Environment, Jimmy. Bubbling over with *Precision* and *Devotion.*

J :   Who could possibly want to work in that type of environment?

R :   No surprise there, Jimmy. *Reliable* and *Honest Brillies* striving to *Accomplish* with a naïve will to be *Accountable.*

J :   Somebody shoot me, please.

R :   You liked *The Wedding Singer* then, Jimmy?

J :   You saw that movie? I can't imagine you liking that one.

R :   Did I say I liked it, Jimmy?

J :   No, I guess not.

R :   Although I must admit, Jimmy, it did have a few good lines in it, especially that song he wrote after he broke up with his fiancée.

J :   That was good, but not exactly a family song, eh?

R :   No, not really, Jimmy.

J :   Now that we have a theme song, can we wrap it up?

R :   Wrap it up with what, Jimmy?

J :   I don't know, ribbons and bows if you like, unless you have a problem with wrapping up?

R :   No problem, Jimmy, as soon as we've finished with *Tangled.*

J :   We're not really using ribbons and bows that can get tangled, we're just—

R :   The movie, Jimmy.

J :   What movie?

R :   *Tangled*, Jimmy. It's about the fairy tale of Rapunzel?

J :   Oh, right. The last fairy tale.

R :   Aye, Jimmy. Always save the best for the last.

J :   It's kind of a cute story, Red, but I don't see Rapunzel being much of a role model.

R :   Not her, Jimmy, the stepmother. Is she not the epitome of *Cross Checking*?

J :   Definitely your kind of TLC for sure.

R :   As you're such a movie buff, Jimmy, I figured you'd have seen that one, in 3D no less.

J :   Yeah. I've seen it.

R :   Well, watch it again then, Jimmy, and take notes.

J :   OK, if I take good notes, will that help me be a super duper?

R :   I think that does it then, Jimmy, unless you have any intelligent questions?

J :   Don't think so, Red. But it's been an eye-opening experience, and I really do appreciate all the time you've spent with me. So what are your plans?

R :   When the book is done, Jimmy, I can use it as a work-book and maybe go on the lecture circuit.

J :   I was actually going to ask about your holidays, but that's a really interesting idea, Red.

R :   I've been toying with this for quite a while now, Jimmy.

J :   Have you done a lot of public speaking then?

R :   None, Jimmy, but I talk to people all the time and some of them even listen.

J :   We're a rare breed, Red. However, I think you just might be a fascinating guest lecturer.

R :   I'm not so sure, Jimmy. I don't think I could ever put people to sleep as effectively as some of the exceptional speakers that I've partially heard at some of the sessions I've attended.

J :   C'mon Red, where's your confidence? I think you'd be better than any of them.

R :   Thanks, Jimmy.

J :   No, really, Red. You'd make a fabulous demotivational speaker, and you can be extremely expiring when you want to be.

R :   Thanks, Jimmy, I appreciate your vote of confidence. I'll certainly consider it if I ever get any offers. Have a very Merry Christmas then, Jimmy.

J :   You too, Red. And don't forget to promote our book when you go out on… tour.

I don't think Red heard most of what I said, as he was already half way up the escalator before the word *tour* slowly dropped off the end of my very dry tongue. I sat there with my mouth still open, wondering if he was serious or not. Would he actually get up in front of an audience and expound upon his bizarre reckonings? I'm sure he'd be a lot more entertaining than any of my Profs.

Suddenly I felt completely disoriented. Were my sessions with Red really over, or might he suddenly reappear on the down escalator and come racing over to tell me he missed something? I don't really know how long I sat there mesmerized by the people descending the down escalator, *waiting*. Red never returned. I suddenly had a brief vision of Rapunzel's mother, the Super Duper witch, and somehow my mind shifted back to my thesis advisor.

To escape the dread of thesis phobia, I became absorbed by all the smiling faces, scurrying away from their Telus Towers weekday prisons, escaping the guarded watch of their respective super dupers. Christmas really is a magical time—a time when Mizzies seem to fade into oblivion.

Chapter VI

The Theisis

The feeling of relief was incredible. My coffee sessions with Red Knech were finally finished. My respite was further magnified by the realization that I was **not** a *Mizzie* after all. The reason I was so certain of this fact was that I had just completed three of the most miserable months of my life, and I had absolutely no interest in ever repeating the experience or anything like it. If I had even the slightest propensity towards leading a *Miz-Life*, apparently I was now cured.

All I had left to do now was complete my thesis, and I could move on with my life in a new direction, somewhere far away from the reckonings of Red Knech. I immersed myself in the task and worked long into the evenings to finish it as soon as possible. I quickly dismissed a twinge of concern that my behaviour appeared to be analogous to that of a workaholic, all of whom are mizzies, according to Red. I attributed my behaviour to the excitement of nearing the finish line, a kind of *man-on-a-mission* fever.

During the next two months I only met with my thesis advisor twice. During my first session, I outlined the premise for my thesis, which generated a rather unenthusiastic response. I listened pensively to my professor's sensitively crafted constructive criticism and desperately attempted to adhere to her suggestions and advice as my thesis evolved. Sincerely believing that the essence of her wisdom was aptly embedded in my masterpiece, I arrived at our next meeting full of anticipation.

Apparently Red was more insightful than I gave him credit for; he and my professor were totally in sync on one specific point—I really wasn't a very good listener. I endured yet another two hours of constructive humiliation and emerged severely demoralized. As I left her office, pulling my tail between my legs so it wouldn't get caught in the door, I came away with a curious nostalgia for my sessions with Red. After all, two hours without a coffee was positively uncivilized, and I had just barely survived my first encounter with a master *Damper*.

At the end of a gruelling month of rewriting and editing, I slowly recovered from a severe case of diminished confidence. When I finally reached a level of comfort that I was ready to defend my thesis, I was full of optimism, and even my professor's cryptic comments barely dented my enthusiasm. Being such a poor listener, it seemed quite possible that I had not clearly understood the real meaning of, *"it's your funeral."* After all, Professors are known to be complex, multi-dimensional thinkers, and their wise council often has hidden meanings that extend well beyond the superficial interpretation of mere words.

As I began to consider the many possible deeper meanings of *"it's your funeral,"* questions flooded my mind. Although we normally associate funerals with death, aren't they sometimes ceremonies that celebrate life? Wasn't my professor of Irish decent? Didn't the Irish refer to a funeral as a wake? And aren't most wakes filled with drinking and merriment? Doesn't the word 'wake' also mean to awaken? Could it not be interpreted as representing a new beginning? The more I considered this, the more convinced I was that my professor's message was one of hope for a fresh start... a new chapter in my life. I decided to defend my thesis.

In retrospect, that may not have been one of my better decisions, but I was at least partially consoled by three factors. The first was that a *'six-month deferral'* is technically not a failure. The second was that I was at least partially correct in the interpretation of my professor's comment; I did get the opportunity for a *'Fresh Start.'* The third was that Red Knech would have absolutely **no** involvement in the next or any other chapter of my life, unless...

The Red Knech Glossary

(Including Some Real Words)

Abdicate	To renounce a responsibility or give up a duty or an obligation
Annoyance Factor	Opposite of Harmony Factor
Brillies	Non Mizzies
Closet Mizzy	Masochists who pretend not to be masochists and who also don't like the word masochist
Demoralize	To debase the morals of; corrupt, to undermine the confidence of; dishearten, to put into disorder; confuse
Equivocate	To use equivocal language intentionally, to speak in ambiguities
Harmony Factor	Opposite of Annoyance Factor
Humiliation Factor	A degree or level of experienced humiliation
I-Ching	The ancient Chinese Book of Change
Intimidate	To make timid, frighten, to discourage or inhibit by threats
Maxi Mizzy	A Mizzy who requires extensive misery to feel fully gratified as a masochist
Mini-Mizzy	A Mizzy who requires only a small amount of misery to feel fully gratified as a masochist
Miz-Addictions	Self-explanatory
Miz-Adventures	Self-Explanatory
Miz-Aptitude	Self-Explanatory
Miz-Atmosphere	Self-Explanatory
Miz-Behaving	Self-Explanatory
Miz-Behavioural types	Self-Explanatory
Miz-Believers	Self-Explanatory
Miz-Benefits	Self-Explanatory
Miz-Content	Self-Explanatory
Miz-Direction	Self-Explanatory
Miz-Dosage	Self-Explanatory
Miz-Dummies	Self-Explanatory
Miz-Effective	Something that is effective from a Mizzy perspective
Miz-Effort	Self-Explanatory
Miz-Enjoyment	Self-Explanatory
Miz-Enthral	Self-Explanatory
Mizerable	Miserable

Mizery	Misery
Miz-Environment	A miserable working environment
Miz-Experience	A miserable experience
Miz-Fitness	Self-Explanatory
Miz-Fortunate	Self-Explanatory
Miz-Genius	Self-Explanatory
Miz-Goals	Self-Explanatory
Miz-Gratification	Self-Explanatory
Miz-Guiding	Self-Explanatory
Miz-Kids	Self-Explanatory
Miz-Leaders	Self-Explanatory
Miz-Leading	Self-Explanatory
Miz-Life	Self-Explanatory
Miz-Logic	Self-Explanatory
Miz-Maintenance	Self-Explanatory
Miz-Management	Miserable Management
Miz-Manger	Manager who is a Mizzy
Miz-mms	Sarcasm, Scepticism, Cynicism, Sardonicism, Pessimism, Nihilism, Negativism, Anarchism, and Syndicalism
Miz-Needs	Self-Explanatory
Miz-Objectives	Self-Explanatory
Miz-Personality	Self-Explanatory
Miz-Progress	Self-Explanatory
Miz-Readers	Self-Explanatory
Miz-Results	Self-Explanatory
Miz-State	Self-Explanatory
Miz-Success	Self-Explanatory
Miz-Successful	Self-Explanatory
Miz-Takes	Mistakes made by Mizzies
Miz-Understanding	Self-Explanatory
Miz-Use	Self-Explanatory
Miz-Virtue	Self-Explanatory
Mizzed-Out	Self-Explanatory
Mizzy	A masochist
Mizzy-Wanna-bees	Self-Explanatory
Obstruct	To block, impede, or hinder an action or operation

Repudiate	To refuse to have anything to do with, to reject the validity of, to disown, to reject, to cast off
Pretend Friend	Two words that rhyme or two people who don't like each other, but pretend to get along, like many in-laws
Prevaricate	To stray from or evade the truth, to walk crookedly, deviate from one's course or path of duty
Second Cup	A chain of Canadian coffee shops started by Frank O'Dea, who is a recovered Mizzy. They are not as well-known as Tim Hortons and their coffee may not be quite as good as Transcends, but they have really friendly staff and great service.
Tergiversate	To change one's mind, subterfuge, to use evasions or ambiguities, to change sides, to turn back
Zan	Contraction of the name Alexandra

The Red Knech Organizer

The Reckonings of Red Knech Organizer								
Chapter	25	24	51	3	27	42	17	21
Character	Abdicator	Tergiversator	Intimidator	Repudiator	Demoralizer	Obstructer	Equivocator	Prevaricator
Name	Dumbper	Jumper	Thumper	Bumper	Damper	Hamper	Stupor	Duper
Manages	Workload	Change	Staff	Clients	Morale	Finance	Production	Ethics
I Ching	The Unexpected	The Turning Point	Shock, Thunder	Difficulty at the Beginning	Providing Nourishment	Increase	Following	Biting Through
Definition	Abdicate	Tergiversate	Intimidate	Repudiate	Demoralize	Obstruct	Equivocate	Prevaricate
	To give up or renounce one's responsibilities	To change one's mind, subterfuge, to use evasions or ambiguities, to change sides, to turn back	To make timid, frighten, to discourage or inhibit by threats	To refuse to have anything to do with, to disown, to reject, to cast off	To debase the morals of; corrupt, to undermine the confidence of; dishearten	To block, impede or hinder an action or operation	To use equivocal language intentionally, to speak in ambiguities	To stray from or evade the truth, to walk crookedly, deviate from one's course
Mizzy Behaviour								
Behaviour	Unreasonable & Irresponsible	Undependable & Disingenuous	Hostile & Callous	Antagonistic & Thoughtless	Disreputable & Arrogant	Disloyal & Obnoxious	Disorganized & Indecisive	Unreliable & Dishonest
Behavioural Practice	BLD	RAT	BAT	RAM	HUB	SOS	VCR	TLC
	Blaming	Reorganizing	Bullying	Rejecting	Humiliating	Stultifying	Vacillating	Trying
	Losing	Adjusting	Annoying	Admonishing	Undermining	Obstructing	Confounding	Lying
	Dumbping	Transforming	Tormenting	Maligning	Berating	Belittling	Rambling	Conniving
Hockey Penalty Analogy	Hooking	Checking	Slashing	Elbowing	High Sticking	Boarding	Tripping	Cross Checking
	Hooking a stick around an opponent to block his progress.	Hitting an opponent whose back is facing you	Hitting an opponent with the stick	Using an elbow in any way to foul an opponent	Striking an opponent while carrying the stick above shoulder level	Shoving an opponent so that he is thrown violently against the boards	Using a stick, knee, foot, arm, hand or elbow to cause an opponent to trip or fall	Hitting an opponent with both hands on the stick
Attitude	Perfidious Negativism	Capricious Pessimism	Contemptuous Sarcasm	Spurious Scepticism	Malicious Sardonicism	Supercilious Nihilism	Fallacious Syndicalism	Mendacious Cynicism
Offence Actions To:	Distress	Stress	Frighten	Insult	Demean	Constrain	Confuse	Frustrate
	Exasperate	Depress	Annoy	Berate	Emasculate	Impede	Confound	Dupe
	Burden	Alienate	Abuse	Defame	Disappoint	Ridicule	Distract	Manipulate
Offence Goals To Change the Environment To be A place where people feel:	Distressed Anguished, Upset, Anxious, Distraught	Stressed Worried, Nervous, Agitated, Tense	Afraid Scared, Fearful, Victimized, Persecuted	Insulted Offended, Harassed, Affronted, Disrespected	Demeaned Humiliated, Degraded, Embarrassed, Diminished	Constrained Unappreciated, Restrained, Constricted, Limited,	Confused Disorganized, Disordered, Incompetent, Disarranged	Frustrated, Discontented, Unfulfilled, Disgruntled, Perturbed
	Exasperated Irritated, Infuriated, Aggravated, Vexed,	Depressed Dispirited, Disheartened, Despondent, Dejected	Annoyed Angry, Provoked, Incensed, Distressed	Berated Rebuked, Criticized, Reproached, Admonished	Emasculated Helpless, Ineffectual, Discouraged, Vulnerable	Impeded Encumbered, Obstructed, Hindered, Hampered	Confounded Baffled, Bewildered, Perplexed, Puzzled	Duped Deceived, Betrayed, Mislead, Deluded
	Exhausted Tired, Fed up, Drained, Worn Out	Alienated Estranged, Ignored, Lost, Irrelevant	Abused Mistreated, Harmed, Injured, Hurt	Defamed Maligned, Denigrated, Disparaged, Badmouthed	Disappointed Dissatisfied, Disillusioned, Disturbed, Saddened	Ridiculed Belittled, Derided, Mocked, Scorned	Distracted Unproductive, Inefficient, Unfocused, Preoccupied	Manipulated, Corrupted, Controlled, Misled, Conned
Red Light	Goals are reached when Miz-mms fill the workplace - Sarcasm, Scepticism, Cynicism, Sardonicism, Pessimism, Nihilism, Negativism, Anarchism, Syndicalism							
Defence Actions To:	Affront	Interrupt	Extort	Ignore	Criticize	Inhibit	Befuddle	Trick
	Provoke	Offend	Browbeat	Slander	Slight	Contradict	Shilly-shally	Cheat
Defence Goals To cause to be:	Contemptible	Unreliable	Belligerent	Dismissed Vilified	Censured	Restricted	Disorganized	Dishonest
	Despicable	Unpredictable	Confrontational		Offended	Obstinate	Incompetent	Deceitful
Red Light	Goals are reached when Perceived with: Disdain, Distrust, Detestation, Denigration, Disrespect, Duplicity, Derision, Deceit							
Mizzy Workplace Objectives Short Term (Atmosphere), Long Term (Environment)								
Atmosphere	Suffocation Repression	Fluctuation Vacillation	Domination Subjugation	Rejection Refutation	Humiliation Deprecation	Debilitation Exacerbation	Disorganization Agitation	Perversion Corruption
Miz-Environment	Exploitive	Disruptive	Oppressive	Depressive	Derisive	Restrictive	Divisive	Deceptive
Brillie (Nemesis) Behaviour								
Behaviour	Reasonable & Responsible	Dependable & Sincere	Affable & Considerate	Congenial & Compassionate	Respectful & Courteous	Loyal & Supportive	Organized & Decisive	Reliable & Honest
Attitude	Infectious Enthusiasm	Ubiquitous Optimism	Sedulous Altruism	Ingenuous Eudemonism	Sagacious Idealism	Industrious Pragmatism	Duteous Devotion	Virtuous Fanaticism
Actions - To:	Achieve	Develop	Lead	Produce	Motivate	Construct	Focus	Accomplish
Goals - To Be:	Successful	Progressive	Inspirational	Responsible	Visionary	Industrious	Decisive	Accountable
Brillie Workplace Objectives Short Term (Atmosphere), Long Term (Environment)								
Atmosphere	Liberation Manumission	Composure Stability	Illumination Communication	Integration Collaboration	Satisfaction Acclamation	Realization Perception	Organization Resolution	Precision Devotion
Environment	Expressive	Productive	Invigorative	Responsive	Positive	Permissive	Cooperative	Supportive

Note from James: Despite strict instructions from Mr. Knech to exclude the above Red Knech Organizer chart on the basis that it denies *Mizzies* the *Miz-Experience* of suffering through the tedious task of doing it themselves. Since it summarizes my entire thesis on one page I added it at the last minute knowing that Mr. Knech would abide by *Miz-Management* principles and approve the book without reading a chart with so much small fine print.

The Red Knech Stickers

Yet another reckoning of Red Knech, on the character of:
James Alden

James Alden was born in a state of naivety in Winnipeg. Although he escaped from Winnipeg several years ago, he seems to have retained his naivety, as he still believes that *Mizzies* are mythical beings. Following his initial exposure to the field of '*Miz-Management*' at the University of Manitoba, he ventured to Oxford for two days where he was not a Rhodes Scholar. He did, however, manage to walk around the campus twice before being escorted off the grounds for reasons not officially recorded. He then set his sights much lower and soon gained complete familiarity with the British form of *Miz-Management* by securing employment as a Red Coat at Butlin's Holiday Camp at Clacton-on-Sea.

Basking in failure, he returned from Europe to further impede his education by not obtaining a Master's in Business at Harvard University. He then concluded his pursuit of virtual learning by not obtaining his PhD in Psychology at Princeton University. Faced with the realization that a fundamental prerequisite to earning a degree requires being accepted into a University and attending classes, he retreated to Edmonton to complete his education as an employee at the University of Alberta.

Although James has never held several positions with such notable companies as Nortel, GroupAction, Briex or JetsGo, he's an internationally un-acclaimed keynote speaker, having neither lectured extensively nor taught countless *Miz-Management* seminars across North America. He has not been a guest lecturer on hundreds of occasions. His numerous unpublished newspaper articles and columns have not inspired millions of *Miz-Managers* nation-wide. He has not written dozens of books on the subject of *Miz-Management* and his unknown works have not made the best-seller list for over thirty continuous weeks. James has not been honoured on several occasions, having not been awarded honorary degrees from three of Canada's most prestigious Universities; Brandon, Laurentian and Lethbridge.

Today, James is not considered to be one of the foremost experts on any subject, especially *Miz-Management*. He has not garnered significant respect in this field, right across Canada, and he has become equally un-respected internationally.

Several motion picture companies have not expressed any interest at all in producing a movie based on his life and experiences.

Although most disgraced recipients of the Order of Canada are normally expected to serve at least some time in in a federal institution, James is confident that he may yet become equally undistinguished and disrespected without ever having to spend any time in Kingston, especially now that Kingston will no longer be an institutional destination.

Backward for Mizzies

If you are a *Mizzy* (a true masochist), please turn to the front of this book and start reading from the very beginning, to obtain the maximum impairment and **do not**, under any circumstance, read beyond this page as it may undo all the injurious effects it may have had on you. Even if you have already read the book, it is recommended that you read it again to capitalize on your *Miz-Experience*.

The end of Book III for Mizzies

If you are a *Brillie* (not a masochist) and you are thumbing through this book trying to figure out why anyone might want to read it...

Hold it... sorry for the interruption...

Mizzies, please stop reading this!

Return to the front of the book, as this epilogue is For Brillies Only!

Seriously, this is really the end for *Mizzies...* nothing more to read here.

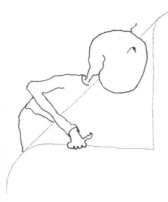

OK, I think they're gone now.

As I was saying, if you are a Brillie (not a masochist) and you are thumbing through this book at a book store, or at a friend's place or in a library (which is highly unlikely, since no libraries carry this book in their collection) and you are trying to figure out why anyone might want to read it... sorry again...

Mizzies, Please don't waste any more of our time. Put the book back...

Mizzies, I asked you nicely to please stop reading this!

Back to the beginning... pleeeeeeze!

ARE THEY GONE?

Is it safe to continue?

Good!

As I was saying to you Brillies, put the book back, and pretend you never saw it!

Unless... perchance you are looking for a book to gift to a pretend friend, who is someone you don't really like very much...?

If that is the case, then maybe this book really is for you, unless the person you are planning to give this book to is actually a *Mizzy*. In either case it won't make much difference, as it is sure to annoy and frustrate the reader, whoever that may be.

On the other hand, there may be one another reason, feeble as it may sound, to read this book. That is if you are some type of Organizational Development Consultant wannabe (or whatever they are called these days), or a really desperate Manager who is more curious than the proverbial cat.

If you suddenly feel an uncontrollable desire to analyze the eight characteristic behaviours to see if there is actually some substance behind the reckonings of Red Knech, or if your curiosity is urging you to consider the inverse of these behavioural patterns to apply them using reverse psychology to possible assist managers to initiate improvements in effectiveness and efficiency in their working environment...

Be very careful!

People are more unpredictable than the weather!

The End of Book III... Really!